FIREPOWER

Kermit Frazier

I0139851

BROADWAY PLAY PUBLISHING INC
New York
www.broadwayplaypublishing.com
info@broadwayplaypublishing.com

First edition: May 2017
I S B N: 978-0-88145-713-1

Book design: Marie Donovan
Page make-up: Adobe InDesign
Typeface: Palatino
Printed and bound in the U S A

FIRPOWER was first produced at the Detroit
Repertory Theatre (Artistic Director, Bruce E Millan) in
Detroit, Michigan, in winter 2017. The cast and creative
contributors were:

GEORGE MONTGOMERY ....David Glover
TYRONE (T C) MONTGOMERY......................Jonathan West
EDWARD (EDDIE) MONTGOMERY.............. William Bryson
ELIZABETH (LIZ) HAL....................................Jennifer Cole
NEIL RUSSELL..Daniel Johnson
JOANNE WELLS ....Casaundra Freeman

Director.. Lynch Travis
Stage manager..Todd Hissong
Set design & construction ....Harry Wetzel
Lighting design ....Thomas Schraeder
Costume design...Sandra Glover
Sound design...Burr Huntington
Lighting technician .... Cornell Marham
Sound technician ....staff
Gallery artist.. Nivet Monet

CHARACTERS & SETTING

GEORGE MONTGOMERY, *African American male, 64 years old*

TYRONE (T C) MONTGOMERY, *African American male, 37 years old*

EDWARD (EDDIE) MONTGOMERY, *African American male, 41 years old*

ELIZABETH (LIZ) HALL, *African American female, 35 years old*

NEIL RUSSELL, *African American male, 27 years old*

JOANNE WELLS, *African American female, 41 years old*

The Time: September 1989
The Place: Washington, D C

ACT ONE

Scene One

(Lights come up center stage on the living room of the MONTGOMERY *home. [Currently in the dark are two smaller spaces: a motel room U R—up right—and a small living room U L—up left—each on a platform raised approximately four feet off the floor.])*

(In the living room center stage, a sofa, easy chair, coffee table, and two end tables are D S [down stage]. A briefcase is on S R [stage right] end table. U R [up right] on side wall is the front door. U C [up center] is a staircase that leads to the second floor, although a wall obscures the banisters starting about halfway up. Just left of the staircase is a mantel on which sit a few family photos and a couple of knick-knacks. Under the mantel is a rectangular table on which is a telephone and stacks of magazines, papers, and other odds and ends, including a leather notebook. S L [stage left] on the side wall is a liquor cabinet. Directly U L [up left] of the mantel is the exit to the dining room and kitchen.)

*(*GEORGE MONTGOMERY, *a 64-year-old African American man, dressed in slacks, a sports jacket, and a dress shirt with no tie, is downing the rest of a can of soda. He sets the can on an end table as* ELIZABETH HALL [LIZ], *a 35-year-old African American woman and* GEORGE's *fiancée, stands nearby. She is dressed in pants and a blouse.)*

(It's a late Sunday afternoon in mid-September, 1989. An upper middle class neighborhood in Washington, D C.)

LIZ: I still think you should wait 'til your son gets home.

GEORGE: He's boo-coo late.

LIZ: And you're doing too much.

GEORGE: I'm doing what I do.

LIZ: Which at the moment is too much.

GEORGE: *(Continuing to search)* Have you seen my notebook?

LIZ: It's on the table under the mantel.

GEORGE: *(Going to the mantel)* Damn. Tell me I'm not going blind now, too.

LIZ: You shouldn't be going anywhere this evening.

GEORGE: I've gotta see McMillan.

LIZ: Tell him to come here.

GEORGE: No, it's my offer. I've got to go to him.

LIZ: Then couldn't you wait 'til—

GEORGE: No. The committee votes Tuesday. He's out of town tomorrow. It's gotta be tonight. *(He stops moving for the first time and just looks at LIZ. Then he smiles and goes to her.)* Look, I'm okay. Really. I'm not feeble or anything. And as far as *last* night's concerned—

LIZ: I don't care about that.

GEORGE: Yes, you do.

LIZ: Why would you say that?

(GEORGE makes a move to turn away but LIZ turns him back to her.)

LIZ: Look at me. I don't care.

GEORGE: Well, you damn sure know I do. Wish there was some magic pill I could take. *(He takes LIZ in his arms and kisses her.)* I love you.

LIZ: Then stay home. Postpone Tuesday's vote.

GEORGE: No. It's now or never.

LIZ: You've said that before.

GEORGE: And this time I mean it. I've been working on different versions of this bill far too long. *(Getting his briefcase)* I still don't see why he wanted to drive here. That's why he's so damn late. Must have bought himself some fancy car he's planning on showing off.

LIZ: He'll need a car when he's here.

GEORGE: Like he couldn't have borrowed one of ours.

LIZ: Not the way we use them all the time.

GEORGE: Well, rented one at the airport then. *(Kissing her again)* I'll be back in a couple of hours or so.

(LIZ gives GEORGE a disapproving look.)

GEORGE: All right, hour and a half. We can have a late dinner.

LIZ: *Here.* We're having it here. We'll even order in if we have to. 'Cause once you get home, Mister, you're not going out again until we go to the hospital in the morning.

(The word "hospital" gives GEORGE pause. Now LIZ kisses him.)

LIZ: In sickness and in health, remember?

GEORGE: Yes, ma'am. I just hope we're not jinxing it by all the time saying it before we actually do it. *(With a wink)* Get married, I mean.

LIZ: You.

(LIZ slaps GEORGE's butt just as he turns away. He gets his briefcase and puts his notebook in it.)

GEORGE: *(Heading to the front door)* And tell that son of mine to keep his ass in this house until I get home. No tipping out of here with whatever so-'n-so he might be aching to see for the first time in months.

LIZ: He's coming to see you.

GEORGE: *(Somewhat skeptically)* Uh-huh. *(He turns around at the door and then flashes a sly smile.)* Who's the one?

(GEORGE's question is the beginning of a familiar exchange between them.)

LIZ: *(Mock seriousness)* That's rhetorical, right?

GEORGE: *(With a wink and a big smile)* Damn straight.

(LIZ smiles. GEORGE exits. She turns D S, takes a moment, and then lets accumulated worry and doubt well up in her.)

(Lights fade to black.)

Scene Two

(Lights come up U R on a hotel room in Washington, D.C. A double bed is U C, a dresser with a mirror over it is U L, and an easy chair is DR. The front door is U R. TYRONE MONTGOMERY [T C], a 37-year-old African American man, dressed just in boxer shorts and socks, is US finishing getting dressed. The rest of his clothes are laid out on the bed; his shoes are on the floor. NEIL RUSSELL, a 27-year-old African American man who actually looks not much older than 21, sits in the easy chair looking through a city guide brochure for Washington, DC. He's already dressed casually.)

(It's later the same Sunday afternoon.)

NEIL: Maybe I'll just ride around on the Metro some. That'll be something new to do. Or go to the zoo. I love me some zoo. Especially aviaries. Birds are bad. Seals are, too. They've got to have the most human faces I've even seen on an animal. And the way they like to play, they could be dogs for mermaids. *(Noticing something in brochure)* Hey, the Vietnam Memorial. That wasn't here last time. Maybe I'll check that out.

(T C continues dressing and checking himself out in the mirror while NEIL continues flipping through the brochure.)

NEIL: Can we at least go out to dinner tonight?

(T C doesn't respond.)

NEIL: Earth to T C.

T C: Yeah, okay.

NEIL: And then maybe to a club. Some damn club.

(His pants and shirt on, T C turns D S to NEIL.)

T C: How do I look?

NEIL: *(With a disinterested glance)* You look all right.

T C: Seriously?

NEIL: *(Into the brochure)* Yeah, man. What's up?

T C: Just stupidly nervous all of a sudden, I guess.

NEIL: I don't see why. It's just gonna be you and your pops.

T C: Not necessarily. His girlfriend, fiancée, whatever, might be there.

NEIL: That's not what I meant.

(T C now knows full well what NEIL means.)

T C: I should bring flowers.

NEIL: Why? Ain't nobody die.

T C: A box of redhots then.

NEIL: Why don't you just wait 'til you get there? See what's what.

T C: No, I've gotta bring him *something*.

NEIL: Yeah, well, you ain't gettin' no help on this end.

(T C *puts on his shoes and continues trying to make himself
look just right.)*

(After some thought)

NEIL: The only other time I've been to D C was on my
senior class trip.

T C: You've told me.

NEIL: Did I tell you I got lost on that trip? Sorta.

T C: No.

NEIL: *(With a laugh)* We were on the Mall near the
Washington Monument. Us and about a million other
folks. And it was pretty hot for spring. We'd been
there most of the day. And man were we ever tired
and hungry. Starting to get all up in each other's faces
and shit. And then somebody begged the teachers to
take us to a *real* mall so that we could at least be cool.
Our teachers powwowed while we just hung out. I was
sorta in the back by myself as usual. Never was one
those class clowns, you know. Despite what you might
think…. Anyway, I'm just standing there waiting when
suddenly I catch the eye of this guy. He's staring at
me. A white guy. In his thirties maybe. Dressed like a
tourist. And when he sees that I'm seeing, he smiles at
me. And I'm thinking, shit, man, is this for real? But
just then this white woman, kinda dumpy, comes up
to him holding a little girl's hand. And just like that it's
gone: the smile, the look, the… whatever. All melted
into the crowd. It was kinda like it didn't happen. He
didn't happen. Like I'd dreamed him up. And when
I came back to myself and turned around, my class
wasn't there anymore. And you know what I did? I
panicked, man. Which was kind of stupid 'cause, shit,
I was seventeen years old, for God's sake, not *seven*.
But I still felt…abandoned. That my classmates and
teachers had deliberately ditched me. I turned around
and around like a damn spinning top, started to get

dizzy, to hyperventilate. And then pow, I saw them. That is, I saw Carrie's flaming-assed red hair. But when I caught up to them it was like nobody had even missed me. Like it didn't really matter whether I was there or not.

(T C senses what NEIL *is really talking about but doesn't want to deal with it.)*

NEIL: Maybe I'm getting too old for you.

T C: What the hell are you talking about?

NEIL: Almost thirty.

T C: You're twenty-seven, for God's sake.

NEIL: I'll be twenty-eight next month.

T C: So?

NEIL: No longer the man of your dreams.

T C: What?

NEIL: Male-patterned baldness kicking in maybe.

T C: I don't—

NEIL: Like my grandfather on my mother's side.

T C: Will you—

NEIL: That's the marker, right?

T C: Stop this.

NEIL: Slobbering all over myself and shit. A damn freaky mutation coming at you!

T C: Stop!

*(*NEIL *stops.)*

T C: You're beautiful. You'll always be beautiful to me.

NEIL: Oh, just beautiful, huh? Not smart or creative or funny—

T C: You know what I mean. I *love* you. *All* of you.

NEIL: *(Pointedly)* Then tell me that in front of your father.

(T C returns to fiddling with his clothes.)

NEIL: Tell me that you love me in front of your father.... Of course, at first I'd have to be *standing* in front of your father. With *you*, I mean. Although I might would even settle for some kind of "third person" love declaration. Me in absentia and shit. "But Dad, I *love* Neil." And since we've never met, me and your father, he's bound to say something like, "Who the hell's Neil?" Which would probably send you stumbling halfway back into yourself again. "Sorry, Dad. *Teneil*. I mean, I love *Teneil*."

T C: We've already gone over this. It was you who insisted on coming anyway.

NEIL: With your proviso that we get a hotel room like you were some damn slinky-assed Congressman or something.

T C: I told you. I'm still not sure how sick he is.

NEIL: And you damn sure don't wanna be responsible for making him sicker.

T C: Look, I haven't seen my father all the much since my mother died. I don't want to be springing everything on him at all once. I thought you understood that.

NEIL: I *do*. I do. Sorta... I just don't fucking *like* it.

(T C goes to NEIL and then hugs and kisses him.)

T C: I know, babe. And I'm really sorry.... That's what you get for hooking up with a half-closeted, cowardly son of a bitch.

NEIL: You're not always a...son of a bitch.

(T C gently shoves NEIL and then prepares to leave.)

T C: Look, even if I wind up having to have dinner with Dad tonight, we can still go clubbing.

NEIL: *(Sarcastically)* Yeah, right. You don't know a club from a golf ball.

(They smile at each other. Then NEIL *kisses* T C.*)*

NEIL: I love you, too, you know. A whole hell of a lot. Which is why if you want my honest opinion, I really don't think you should be wearing that shirt with those pants.

T C: I thought you said I looked all right.

NEIL: For a middle-aged nerd.

T C: I'm not middle-aged.

NEIL: You want me to dress you?

T C: Yeah, you'd like that.

NEIL: Just shut up and take off either the pants or the shirt.

(T C takes a moment and then begins taking off his pants.)

(Lights fade to black.)

Scene Three

(Lights come up U L on the living room of JOANNE WELLS' *house in the Anacostia section of Washington, D C. There is a sofa and coffee table D C and an easy chair D L. The front door is U L.* JOANNE, *a 41-year-old African American woman, is sitting on the sofa and speaking on a cordless telephone.)*

(It's the same late Sunday afternoon.)

JOANNE: When did he come home?… Where's he been for two days? …Doing what, for heaven's sake?…

(EDWARD MONTGOMERY [EDDIE], *a 41-year-old African American man, enters S L and goes to the entrance to the house. He's dressed in a manner that's a little out of style for the late 1980s. He carries a backpack over his left shoulder. With some apprehension he rings the doorbell.* JOANNE *looks toward the door.*)

JOANNE: Okay, Mrs Greer, I understand…. Yes, of course, I'll come by tomorrow…. Yes, in the afternoon, after school. Please, see that he goes to school.

(EDDIE *rings the doorbell again.*)

Listen, I've got somebody at my door…. No, no, that's all right. That's what I'm here for. I'm just glad he came back. We'll deal with the other stuff later. I'll give you a call in the morning…. Yes, you take care now.

(JOANNE *hangs up the phone, sighing deeply. Then she goes to the door and opens it. She is truly shocked to see* EDDIE.)

EDDIE: Hi, Joanne… Can I come in?

(JOANNE *isn't sure. Finally she steps aside and motions* EDDIE *to enter. He does so and she closes the door.*)

EDDIE: Is this a bad time?

(JOANNE *says nothing.*)

EDDIE: I knew you were gonna be surprised to see me. But I didn't wanna call first because… .

(EDDIE *and* JOANNE *both know the reason.*)

EDDIE: You look really good.

(JOANNE *rolls her eyes.*)

EDDIE: I've really missed you.

JOANNE: Don't, Eddie. Don't you dare go there.

EDDIE: It's the truth.

(JOANNE *moves away from* EDDIE *and around the room, as though trying to get her bearings. Then she finally stops and turns to him.*)

JOANNE: How'd you even know I'd moved back to D C?

EDDIE: Warren Redman told me a couple of months ago. Said you came back home to take care of your mother. That she passed away last year. Sorry for that.

JOANNE: Thank you.... I suppose you're back in town to see your father.

EDDIE: Why would you say that? He don't wanna see me. I came back to see *you.*

JOANNE: Then you don't know.

EDDIE: Know what?

JOANNE: Your father's got...cancer.

(EDDIE *is taken aback.*)

JOANNE: Starts radiation treatment tomorrow.

EDDIE: What kind of cancer?

JOANNE: Prostate.

(*Again* EDDIE *takes a moment to take in the news.*)

EDDIE: How do you know all this?

JOANNE: Girlfriend of mine. Co-worker.... She's "close" to your father.

(EDDIE *understands.*)

(*Slight pause*)

JOANNE: So...you came all the way back home from who-knows-where just to see me.

EDDIE: What's the matter with that?

(JOANNE *purses her lips, waits.*)

EDDIE: Okay, all right. I've got a little something in the works, too.

JOANNE: You haven't changed a bit, have you, Eddie?

EDDIE: What's that supposed to mean?

(JOANNE *says nothing.*)

EDDIE: Yeah, I've changed. Changed a hell of a lot. And like I said, and it's the God's honest truth, I really, really missed you. The whole time.

JOANNE: Even when you got married in California and had a daughter and got divorced and never seemed to call. Is that part of that "whole time" you're talking about?

EDDIE: I got wrapped up, okay? After that first summer back home, when we did all those things, made all those plans, I went back out to California and got too wrapped up, swallowed up.

JOANNE: And me back in D C just working and waiting.

EDDIE: It wasn't like I didn't think about you a lot. It was more like I was working so hard to keep my ass from drownin'. And it was like Eddie this and Eddie that. Eddie, Eddie, Eddie. And then this one girl—

(JOANNE's *expression of disgust stops* EDDIE *for a moment.*)

EDDIE: Then Melinda got pregnant and I thought getting married was the right thing to do. Get married, have the kid, be a man. And then tryin' to go pro with a family in tow. Rocket for an arm just like my dad, and they want me to play cornerback like all I was was legs and moves. And then my damn knee went out. Twice. And suddenly I'm expendable. Gotta get me a regular-assed job. And I looked around and saw how white my world had become. Found myself spending more and more time with the brothers in South Central. Cracked my marriage wide open.

But I couldn't come back home. I was too ashamed. Tail between my legs like some ole beaten down performing monkey. Besides, you were hitched and gone yourself by then. So I just gradually booked on out of the country to Canada, then Morocco, then across Gibraltar to Spain. Odds and ends in Spain. Hell, you'd be surprised how easy it is to slip into this image of yourself as some sorta sapped-out expatriate. Some beat-down writer or some jazz musician who'd hocked his horn. Or better yet some black power burnout. Especially with my Eldridge Cleaver goatee. And now...back home.

(JOANNE *eyes* EDDIE's *backpack.*)

JOANNE: I hope you're not gonna to tell me that everything you own now is in that backpack.

EDDIE: *(Easing his backpack off his shoulder)* Naw.

(JOANNE *watches carefully as* EDDIE *sets the backpack down as though he's making a play to stay.*)

EDDIE: Got a couple of bags in a storage locker at the Greyhound.

JOANNE: Where're you staying?

(EDDIE *just looks at* JOANNE. *Finally...*)

EDDIE: *(Lying)* Oh, I'm gonna be crashing at Warren's. He's got a crib out near Benning Road. Been there since his wife split with their kids half a dozen years ago.

JOANNE: Huh. Ain't it the way.

EDDIE: *(Picking up his backpack)* Anyway, I just wanted to see how you were doing? And I guess you're doing just fine…. I better get going. *(He turns to go.)*

JOANNE: Are you…

(EDDIE *turns back with some anticipation.*)

JOANNE: Are you going to look in on your dad?

EDDIE: Hell, I don't know. He's gonna be fine, too, I'm sure. Besides, I don't think him seeing me now is any recommended part of his treatment. *(He just looks at* JOANNE *for a long while. Finally…)* I still love you, you know.

JOANNE: I heard that…. And I've heard it before.

*(*EDDIE *exits.* JOANNE *is unsure of what she feels about him now.)*

(Lights fade to black.)

Scene Four

(Lights come up on the Montgomery living room. No one is there. T C enters S R carrying a small gift bag and dressed in a light jacket and pants that much better match his shirt. He goes to the entrance to the house. With some apprehension he rings the doorbell. After a moment LIZ *enters U L from the dining room/kitchen and crosses to the front door. She opens it.)*

(It's early evening.)

LIZ: Oh, my goodness gracious, you must be Tyrone.

T C: Yep, it's me.

LIZ: Well, come on in. Welcome home.

T C: *(Entering)* Thanks.

*(*LIZ *and T C hug somewhat awkwardly.)*

LIZ: I'm Liz Hall.

T C: That's sorta what I figured.

LIZ: Right. Of course…. Your father's told me so much about you. He's so proud of you.

T C: How's he doing?

LIZ: Pretty good under the circumstances. In fact, he had to step out earlier to attend an emergency meeting. City council matters.

T C: Still so busy.

LIZ: Takes his public service very seriously.

T C: *(Holding up gift bag)* I brought him something. Some redhots. Don't know if he can have them, but they're his—

LIZ: Favorite candy. I know. *(She takes the bag and puts it on an end table.)* Where're your bags? I thought you planned to stay the week.

T C: I do.... I've got a hotel room.

LIZ: Why in the world would you get a hotel room?

T C: I just thought...well, you and Dad—

LIZ: Hey, now, quiet as it's kept, we only use one of the three bedrooms. Your brother's old bedroom is your father's home office now, and we've been using the other one as sort of a guest room since last spring, but it's still yours.

T C: Kathy's.

LIZ: I beg your pardon.

T C: It was Kathy's room. At least that's sometimes how I remember it. Me and Eddie shared a bedroom when we first moved here, just like we did in Anacostia. But when Kathy died, well, Eddie wanted his own room. He was thirteen, this big-time teenager, and I was only nine. *(With a laugh)* Not even a double-digit dude yet, he said. So I moved into Kathy's room. Spent a whole year not wanting my friends to come over, especially to sleep over. So afraid that they'd tease me about being in a "girl's" room. Took Mom and Dad that long to finally change the colors. A whole year sleeping in sort of a shrine.

LIZ: I didn't know.

T C: Was a long, long time ago.

LIZ: Well, anyway, stop this foolishness and check out of that hotel.

T C: I can't right now.

LIZ: Why not?

T C: I need to speak to Dad first.

LIZ: Are you sure this doesn't have anything to do with me?

T C: No, Elizabeth—

LIZ: Liz, please.

T C: Liz. It's not about you.

(LIZ says nothing more.)

T C: *(Reluctantly)* I'm not alone.

LIZ: Oh, come on now, Tyrone. Is that all? So the two of you can use your old room. This *is* 1989, you know.

T C: I know.

LIZ: Then what's the problem?

(T C feels incapable of taking the next step. Then suddenly something occurs to LIZ.)

LIZ: Oh…. She's white.

T C: I…

LIZ: Yes, I heard about what your brother went through with your dad when he married a white woman. But that was what? Twenty years ago? And as for me, even though I know the cliché rant sisters make about a third of the black men being in jail and another third being—

T C: She's a he.

LIZ: *(Taken aback)* Oh, I see.

T C: Which I guess makes me a part of that second "third."... He's black, though. Does that make it better?

LIZ: Not statistically. *(Pause)* So your father doesn't know.

T C: No. As matter of fact, you're probably the first person in all of D C to know.

LIZ: Well...that's some honor.

T C: Look, I really didn't expect it to go this way. I just wanted to tell him first. If not today then maybe tomorrow, or the next day. But I want to tell him before I...show him.

LIZ: Why show or tell him at all?

T C: Come again?

LIZ: That is, right now. With his radiation treatments starting, with the stress of all that.

T C: It's not my intention to hurt him any more than he might already be hurting. I just want to be honest with him about all this for once. *(Pause)* I suppose you'd like to renege on your insisting that I stay in the house where I grew up.

LIZ: You're the one who booked a hotel room.

T C: Let's just say that I needed a staging area for my assault on his sensibilities.

LIZ: Please, don't make me out to be the enemy. We just met.

T C: I'm not. I just want to do this right.

LIZ: Which is why I suggest that you wait 'til his treatments are over.

T C: No.

LIZ: What's two more months after however many years?

T C: A hell of a lot more than you know…. Three years ago I wanted to tell my mother. Wanted to tell her first. But then that summer she got sick. Boom, just like that. Stomach ache, check up, stage four colon cancer. Gone in six weeks. And every time I'd go to the hospital to see her, to see her in so much pain…

(GEORGE *enters S R carrying his briefcase and goes to the entrance to the house.*)

LIZ: But your dad's going to be all right.

T C: How do you know that?

LIZ: Because he's strong.

T C: So was my mom.

(GEORGE *puts his key in the door and enters.*)

GEORGE: Well, finally.

T C: Hi, Dad.

GEORGE: *(Closing the door)* So where's your spanking new Mercedes?

T C: Huh?

LIZ: Your father thought the reason you weren't flying out was that you'd bought a new car you wanted to show him.

T C: On a college professor's salary?

GEORGE: Who else you got to be spending it on, Mister Still Footloose and Fancy Free? *(Setting down his briefcase)* Come here, you.

(GEORGE *and* T C *come toward each other,* GEORGE *noticeably less spry than he was when he left the house earlier. They embrace.*)

GEORGE: It sure is good to see you, son.

T C: It's good to see you, too, Dad. How you feeling?

GEORGE: None the worse for wear.

T C: You look good.

GEORGE: I'm putting on weight. These damn monthly Lupron shots. It's like I'm turning into one of those middle-aged men who leads with his stomach.

T C: Not too far. I mean, so far. I mean—

GEORGE: You're *supposed* to say, "No you're not". ... Anyhow, at least my blood pressure's steady and I haven't started breaking any bones yet. *(Looking toward* LIZ*)* Liz has been taking good care of me. I told her I was going to kick your butt good if you didn't get here soon, you know.

T C: Accident on the Pennsylvania Turnpike.

GEORGE: Worse stretch of road in the whole Northeast. *(Looking around)* I must have just missed you when I left out of here earlier.

T C: How do you mean?

GEORGE: I don't see your bags, which means they must be already upstairs in your room.

T C: No, I... .

LIZ: *(To the rescue)* His bags are still in his car.

GEORGE: What for? You wanted to make sure your ole man hadn't already keeled over or something?

LIZ: George.

GEORGE: I'm just messin' with him, Liz. *(Bear-hugging* T C*)* T.C. knows that. I've always liked messin' with him.

T C: Yeah, 'cause you knew I was the only one of your sons who'd stand for it.

GEORGE: Don't be selling yourself short. You're the one who stuck to where you were heading.

(Slight pause)

(Both GEORGE *and* T C *are thinking about* EDDIE.*)*

T C: Have you heard from—

GEORGE: No.

(Slight pause)

LIZ: How'd your meeting go?

GEORGE: We agreed on principle. But we'll see come Tuesday.

T C: Tuesday?

GEORGE: Big housing vote. *My* bill. *(To* LIZ*)* How about dinner?

LIZ: I'm in the middle of making a salad.

GEORGE: I thought we were—

LIZ: To go along with making a phone call to Sonny Jim's Barbecue.

*(*LIZ *sneaks* T C *a look of both sympathy and warning and then exits U L to the kitchen.)*

GEORGE: Yeah, I know, your mother would never have even thought about ordering take-out for Sunday dinner.

T C: It's okay, Dad.

(There's an awkward moment between GEORGE *and T C, as though each were waiting for the other to say something. Finally…)*

GEORGE: She's thirty-five.

T C: Dad, I don't care.

GEORGE: Nevertheless, I've found it best to get it out of the way with some folk right up front.

T C: I'm not "some folk."

GEORGE: Yeah, I know. Although sometimes it seems like that the way you've been staying away from home lately.

T C: I know, Dad, I'm sorry…. Where'd you and Liz meet?

GEORGE: At a D C statehood rally. She's really interested in local politics, although she's a social worker by profession.

T C: Must help that you're a big-time city councilman then. *(Immediately backtracking)* That came out wrong.

GEORGE: It's okay. I can take it. For the record, she owns a condo and has her own pension plan.

T C: Dad, I—

GEORGE: And on top of that, we really do love each other.

T C: I'm sure you do.

GEORGE: Of course, don't get me wrong 'cause I also loved your mother very, very much. She was like nobody else. *Nobody.* And nobody'll ever be able to replace her either.

T C: Will you stop. I'm happy you found somebody. And I know that Mom would be happy for you, too.

GEORGE: Thanks. That means a lot.

T C: *(Getting redhots)* Oh, here. Didn't know if you were allowed to have them but—

GEORGE: Hey, now, hormone therapy don't change everything about me, you know. I'm still a man…who likes his redhots. *(Taking the redhots)* Thank you.

T C: You're welcome.

(While GEORGE *exams the box of redhots,* T C *tries to work his way up to coming out to him.)*

T C: Dad…there's something I need to—

GEORGE: We plan on having kids, you know.

T C: Oh?

GEORGE: Yeah. Liz wants kids of her own. And I want what she wants.

T C: Are you sure?

GEORGE: Of course, I'm sure.

(T C *is hesitant to speak.*)

GEORGE: What, you think I'm too old?

T C: No, it's not that.... Is that why you opted not to have a prostatectomy?

(GEORGE *is surprised.*)

T C: I've been reading up.

GEORGE: Then you must also know that taking out the prostate doesn't necessarily mean that you get all the cancer. And I'd have to undergo this chemical castration shit regardless, the point being to kill your testosterone so it can't feed the cancer cells. Which seems like some damn sick joke if you ask me: a man being punished for being too male. And ain't no way in hell I'm ever gonna have them cutting off my balls.

T C: Why do you have to put it that way?

GEORGE: All right, testicles, then. Is that a better way? Hell, the damn biopsy was hard enough. The whole time they were digging down there I kept thinking about that story your grandfather told me about a neighbor of his in South Carolina getting lynched. How they'd cut off his privates and stuffed them in his mouth.... Okay, so maybe I *am* being too sensitive, too irrational. But why is it that this kind of cancer is more common with us? Answer me that.

T C: In this country, you mean.

GEORGE: Yeah, well, this is where we've been for four hundred years. It's like it's some sort of medical conspiracy. One more way to castrate the black man. What with Tuskegee and AIDS and—

T C: AIDS isn't a conspiracy, Dad. You know that.

GEORGE: No, I don't know that. There's a lotta things
we don't know about it. Except maybe that it might as
well be a death sentence. But hey, all right. You might
be right. Long as hard drugs and gay sex aren't your
thing then...

(T C *says nothing.*)

GEORGE: Anyway, enough "dirty talk". Go get your
bags.

T C: *(Preoccupied)* What?

GEORGE: You can see your ole man's not dead, so bring
your bags on in here. Stay for more than a minute.
(Calling U L) When's the barbecue coming, Liz?

LIZ: *(Calling)* About fifteen minutes. *(Entering)*

The salad's done, though.

GEORGE: The rabbit food can wait. *(He goes U L to the
liquor cabinet.)* First, we've got to make a toast. *(He takes
out a bottle of wine and three glasses.)*

LIZ: Not the evening before your treatments start.

GEORGE: *(Pouring the wine)* Hell, a sip of vino won't
hurt. Let's just call it a treat before the treat... ment.
Besides, my oh so successful college professor son's in
town.

(GEORGE *gives glasses of wine to* LIZ *and* T C.)

LIZ: Well, if you promise to have only this one little
glass. *(Raising her glass)* Here's to the beginning of
George Montgomery's successful radiation therapy.

T C: *(Raising his glass)* Here, here!

GEORGE: *(Raising his glass)* And here's to this boy's
having somebody in our wedding party next June who
can catch the damn bridal bouquet.

(As they clink glasses T C *smiles somewhat painfully, while* LIZ *isn't sure how to react.)*

(Lights fade to black.)

Scene Five

(Laughter is heard as the lights come up U L on JOANNE's *living room.* JOANNE *and* LIZ *are hanging out, drinking red wine, and munching on chips.)*

(It's evening of the next day: Monday.)

LIZ: No, he didn't tell him. George was pretty tired out after dinner so I insisted that he go to bed. And T C took that opportunity to drive back to his hotel and get a bag of clothes. So he stayed in his old room, after all. Just alone.

JOANNE: *(Shaking her head)* Um, um, um. Little T C.

LIZ: When *I* was little I remember my aunt used to refer to a certain great uncle as "funny". I thought that meant he was always telling jokes or something. And when I first saw him at a family reunion some of my cousins did tend to laugh at him behind his back. They'd imitate the way he walked and moved his hands. So then I figured that that's what my aunt meant by funny, although to me he just looked sorta happy. But finally this ole bullet-head of a cousin named Rufus, who had the biggest ole owl eyes I'd ever seen, took me aside and started talking about nasty stuff some men did with other men. And I kinda went "eww" and sorta got it. Although I've gotta say that Rufus was a whole lot funnier looking than that great uncle.

JOANNE: Meaning Rufus was just plain ugly, not gay.

LIZ: "Gay" also means profligate, licentious.

JOANNE: According to who?

LIZ: Look it up.

JOANNE: I don't think the word "gay" is in the Bible that way.

LIZ: The dictionary.

JOANNE: That's usage, girl.

LIZ: I know, I know. Nevertheless, I still don't approve.

JOANNE: Oh, come on now, Liz. If it's who he is, it's who he is. You don't have to approve of it, just tolerate it.

LIZ: Yeah, that's we black folks, all right. Conservative approvers. Liberal toleraters. Sure makes for one hell of a yin-yang in and out of church on Sundays, though.

JOANNE: That's for sure. *(Imitating a church elder)* "Lawd, please, please save Brother Johnson, but don't you be fooling with that powerful singing voice."

(JOANNE and LIZ laugh.)

LIZ: *(Soberly)* It could also help fuel a political hot bed for George.

JOANNE: In what way?

LIZ: He's coming out against some gay rights legislation.

JOANNE: Why?

LIZ: 'Cause he needs that housing bill of his to become law. You know how bad things are for some of us. Especially here in Anacostia.

JOANNE: You don't have to be telling me.

LIZ: Anyway, that bill's the linchpin of his run for city council next fall. And in order to get his bill he needs Councilman McMillan's support and to get that he's gotta give up something.

JOANNE: Do you really think that's wise?

LIZ: In politics compromise is often wise.

JOANNE: No, I mean for him to be running again, under the circumstances.

LIZ: He wants a second term. He deserves it. And as far as I'm concerned being for family values is a plus. It puts him right in line with the coalition of ministers who've always supported him as well as with his constituents, especially those in Anacostia where he's still got strong ties.

JOANNE: You mean he's gonna forego his At-Large seat for the one in Ward Eight?

LIZ: No, that seat's not up until '92.

JOANNE: *(Sarcastically)* Well, that must be a relief.

LIZ: What's that supposed to mean?

JOANNE: Otherwise, you'd have to be moving back on "across the river" again like me.

LIZ: Look, I make no apologies for liking it up there. Nice and quiet. Close to Rock Creek Park. Besides, you know how much Anacostia's changed since it morphed into Ward Eight.

JOANNE: That's 'cause all you middle class black folks abandoned it.

LIZ: It's called "movin' on up," girl.

JOANNE: Oh, not "movin' on out?"

LIZ: Now, *that's* usage.

(JOANNE *and* LIZ *laugh.*)

LIZ: Anyway, for those who've stayed, it's George Montgomery and Marion Barry all the way.

JOANNE: In that order, huh?

LIZ: Oh, yeah. George is my man. Smart, accomplished, charismatic.

JOANNE: I heard that now.

(*Suddenly,* LIZ *grows serious.*)

JOANNE: What's wrong?

LIZ: It was harder than I thought it would be today.
Never really spent all that much time in hospitals.
But believe it or not I wanted to be a doctor when I
was growing up. I had myself curing dolls right and
left. Then things got tight at home in high school and
I "downshifted" to nurse. Then organic chemistry
kicked my butt real good in college and I thought:
hmm, social work. Now there's a "helping" profession
for "mathephobics". I don't have to be curing the
damn dolls, just makin'em get along. Huh, little did I
know that'd be just another complex kind of organic
chemistry.

JOANNE: It suits you well enough.

LIZ: Suits the both of us, girl.

JOANNE: I'm not so sure about me these days. It's like I
can smell a burnout coming.

LIZ: The Jamal Gatlin case?

JOANNE: Yeah. When I sat him down to talk all he
wanted to do was gripe about curfews and clothes and
pocket change. I told him if he aged out of the system
before he finished high school there'd be a whole new
set of "problems" for him to face.

LIZ: And?

JOANNE: He pouted and half-nodded and promised
to do better. But he's still incredibly angry. Angry at
his father for being in jail, at his mother for being on
drugs, at the whole damn world.

LIZ: You've had worse cases.

JOANNE: I know. But it's gotten me all of a sudden thinking about Damien. Wondering if he thinks I've abandoned *him*.

LIZ: You've got to raise up behind that thought, girlfriend. Besides, I thought he liked being at Saint Paul's.

JOANNE: He does. Or at least he did. In fact, he begged me to let him go. "Mom, I don't like the school I'm at." Said he was being treated like a punk for acting "too white."

LIZ: Then you did the right thing by sending him.

JOANNE: Yeah, but when he came back from staying with his father for three weeks last summer, suddenly he wasn't so sure.

LIZ: Well, your "ex" is no expert.

JOANNE: Oh, he's an expert, all right. That's why he's an "ex". And the way that boy was beginning to swagger around here and hang out more with his new "peeps"... Well, I was afraid that—

LIZ: Damien's not like that, and you know it.

JOANNE: He's a teenager. Which means he could be a half a dozen things I don't know about.

LIZ: You're doing the right thing. Besides, you're a black parent with a young son. What's that sober little couplet Randall came up with at last year's retreat? "Basic rule for black boys when stopped by the police: Keep your eyes on the prize and your hands open wide."

(JOANNE *and* LIZ *let that sink in.*)

LIZ: Anyway, I'd give almost anything to be having a son or daughter like Damien.

JOANNE: So then you're still sticking to your "family plan."

LIZ: Yeah, I guess. Thanks to George's "sperm bank account." *(Laughing)* Deposits and withdrawals. *(Soberly)* Am I being too selfish?

JOANNE: You've got a right to think about yourself.

LIZ: That's not what I asked?

JOANNE: Isn't it?

LIZ: But what if the radiation treatment fails? Or if it's successful, what if his cancer comes back?

JOANNE: You'll deal with it.

LIZ: Is he too old?

JOANNE: No.

LIZ: 'Cause I've been burned too many damn times by men my age. Steppin' up strong and then tippin' out with the goods.

JOANNE: He's not too old.

LIZ: I knew he was twice my age from the jump. Knew how it might look. But it felt so good, you know. The sound of that voice at that statehood rally. *(Imitating* GEORGE*)* "It's about us being in charge of our own affairs, our own destiny." *(Back to herself)* The look in his eyes when they first landed on me. That first dinner. Then the second. Then the kisses good night. Then the whole thing. And then suddenly, like out of nowhere…. And the medication makes it tough. Don't wanna complain. He's got enough to deal with. But in bed, wanting him the way it was, inside me…. Thinking about that child I wondered if I'd ever have. Never wanting to be like half my clients yet still wanting to be like…you.

JOANNE: Come on now.

LIZ: He's got two grown sons.

JOANNE: He wants you.

LIZ: I know that. I can feel it in the way he still holds me. But do I still want him? That is, well...hell, I don't want to wind up being a nurse maid. Or a single mother.

JOANNE: Like me, you mean.

LIZ: You're a divorced mother.

JOANNE: Who was virtually a single mother even when she was married.... More wine?

LIZ: No, thanks.

(JOANNE *pours herself more wine and takes a sip as* LIZ *simply watches her carefully.*)

LIZ: You've still got a serious thing for him, don't you?

JOANNE: Who, my ex?

(LIZ *simply waits.*)

JOANNE: Oh, you mean Eddie?

(Again, LIZ *says nothing.)*

JOANNE: I don't know.... No...yes. It's not a fair question.

LIZ: Why not?

JOANNE: 'Cause the answer can't be rooted in the rational.

LIZ: Well, ta-ta for you, Ms Rational.

(JOANNE *sighs deeply.*)

JOANNE: My first really "true love". And then he ups and breaks my heart into more pieces that I can count. And it wasn't just that she was white, or that she was pregnant. It was the simple fact that she wasn't me.

LIZ: Oh, it wasn't that she was white, huh?

JOANNE: Do we always have to go there?

LIZ: As long as there's a "there" to go to, we'll steady be going to it, I think. *(Slight pause)* Are you going to see him again?

JOANNE: You sound like we went on a date last night.

LIZ: Are you?

JOANNE: I don't know where he is.

LIZ: I thought he was staying with some friend of his.

JOANNE: I don't have his number.

LIZ: Don't you know his name?

JOANNE: Stop pressuring me.

LIZ: Stop being so chicken.

JOANNE: What good would it do? He's still like some unfulfilled, excuse-ridden, overgrown adolescent in many ways.

LIZ: You mean he's like every other man on the planet, black, white, or green.

JOANNE: He also doesn't seem to have a profession, or even a job.

LIZ: You're no pushover.

JOANNE: I don't want to wind up being a nurse maid any more than you do.

LIZ: Touché. *(She eyes the bottle of wine.)* On second thought, I think I *will* have a little more wine.

(JOANNE pours wine for LIZ.)

(Lights fade to black.)

Scene Six

(Lights come up U R on the hotel room. T C and NEIL *enter, both a little high and nearly falling over each other with giddiness, having just come from a gay club—the first for each of them in D C.)*

(It's just after midnight—very early Tuesday morning.)

T C: *(A finger to his lips)* Shh.

NEIL: Why? Hell, we're in a royal house of… assignation, sir.

T C: "Assignation." Shit, teach you a word and you wanna use it to death.

NEIL: Hey, back up Professor Higgins. *(With some flair)* 'Cause this diva's got much more goin' on than Ms Eliza ever had.

T C: I don't do divas.

NEIL: That's so sad.

T C: I think I'm a little drunk.

NEIL: No kidding. At least it finally got you out on the dance floor. I don't go to clubs just to profile and gawk.

T C: Was I that bad?

NEIL: Just in the gawking department, actually. I think I profiled enough for the both of us.

T C: You know how much I hate '70s retro music.

NEIL: Good times, babe, good times. And you can't tell me you didn't do even one private little disco dance to Miss Diana's *I'm Coming Out* way back when.

T C: Didn't I just tell you I don't do divas? Besides, "times" have changed.

NEIL: Yeah, I could see it in some of the faces. The music barely a cover. Spinning and dancing. Around and around and around you go and where you stop…

nobody knows. Who to touch, who to trust, who to talk to, cling to. Which is why I'm oh so glad I've got you.

(NEIL *kisses* T C.)

T C: We've got each other.

(T C *kisses* NEIL.)

NEIL: Hey, hey, I know. Why don't we just pack up all our stuff, drive over to your house, and sneak up to your room? I'm just dying to see that "girl's room" of yours.

T C: It's not a girl's room anymore, I told you.

NEIL: Oh, right. At least not since you stopped living at home.

T C: Fuck you.

NEIL: Pretty please.

T C: Whoa, whoa, stop it, before we become every other straight person's worst gaydar nightmare.

NEIL: Straight people don't have no gaydar.

T C: Yeah, they do. It's just so God-awfully narrow and naïve. On top of that, they don't wanna have to be thinking about what they think that they think that they know that we do.

NEIL: Ha! Leave it to you to try pussy-footing your way around a fabulous fuck.

(NEIL *and* T C *fall into each other's arms onto the bed hugging and kissing. Then they grow serious.*)

NEIL: Still, it's scary.

T C: Yeah.

NEIL: And it's not going away, is it?

T C: I don't know. (*After a moment he perks up and laughs.*)

NEIL: What's so funny?

T C: I still can't believe you got carded again.

NEIL: Well, it ain't my fault. It's genetic and shit.

T C: And you thought you were getting too old.

NEIL: I didn't say I thought that I was getting too old. I said I thought I was getting too old for *you*.

T C: *(With a kiss)* Never, babe.

NEIL: Besides, you should just be happy nobody accused me of being your rent boy the way that mean, muscle-shirted hustler did last month in Chicago.

(Unhappy with that memory, T C pushes up and away from NEIL.)

NEIL: Hey, come on, T C. Why should you care? I don't.

T C: Then why bring it up?

NEIL: To mess with you. You know I like messing with you. 'Cause you're so eminently "mess-withable."

T C: You sound like my father.

NEIL: Well, he's got *hisself* a "young honey" now so why shouldn't you?

T C: A homophobic young honey.

NEIL: You don't know that for sure. She might just be protecting you.

T C: From who?

NEIL: Your father.

T C: Like she knows him better than I do.

NEIL: She might.

(T C considers this.)

NEIL: On the other hand, he might already know.

T C: I doubt that.

NEIL: Well, listen to you, Miss Queen of the Airtight Closet.

T C: That's "Mister King" to you, sir.

NEIL: All I know is *my* parents knew by the time I hit high school.

T C: That's 'cause you insisted on hitting them over the head with it.

(T C *playfully bops* NEIL *over the head. Then they kiss and cuddle together again.*)

NEIL: So… I'm coming with you tomorrow morning, right?

T C: *(Caught off guard)* I said I'd think about it.

NEIL: No, that's what you said after coming back from a *second* dinner with your father without me. At the club you said okay.

T C: At the club I was…high.

NEIL: *(Pulling up and away)* Oh, and now you're oh so low again. Down low, I mean. You're getting more and more like Joel.

T C: Joel was married with two kids…. And I'm better looking.

(NEIL *just sulks.*)

T C: Come back here.

NEIL: No.

T C: Please.

(NEIL *goes back to* T C.)

NEIL: What do you want?

T C: Remember…remember when we first met?

NEIL: Hey now, I don't hear no violins playin' so you can stop that tactic right—

T C: *(A finger to* NEIL's *lips)* Wait, wait…. I'd never flat-out fallen in love with anybody before you. Not once. Oh, I mean I loved my parents and brother and sister and grandparents and all, but I didn't <u>fall</u> in love with them. And I'd never ever had that feeling about any girl I went out with, much less allow myself to think about having it about any guy. Shit, my first out-and-out, heart-pounding, can't-hardly-work-without-thinking-about-you-or-sleep-without-dreaming-about-you love. And I thought, yeah, it's okay. It's pretty goddamn okay.

(T C *bops* NEIL *playfully on the nose with a finger this time.* NEIL *smiles.)*

T C: How about I pick you up in the afternoon?

NEIL: No, uh-uh.

T C: Come on, babe.

NEIL: I don't think so.

T C: Why not?

NEIL: Because it'll probably be too late by then.

T C: What do you mean?

NEIL: I might well be on a flight back to O'Hare.

T C: But…how would you get to the airport?

NEIL: What, you think I'm twelve?

T C: Okay, okay, calm down.

NEIL: I'm perfectly calm. And now I'm oh so clear-eyed, too.

T C: We'll spend just one more night here.

NEIL: You mean I'll spend just one more night here.

T C: We'll check out tomorrow morning after I get back from my dad's treatment.

NEIL: Now you see, that's the problem right there. Your dad's treatment. *His* treatment. Not yours.

T C: But—

NEIL: I'm not going through this shit again.

T C: And I tell you I'm not *Joel*.

NEIL: The fuck you aren't.

T C: Look, just 'cause your father skipped out on you doesn't mean I don't care about my own.

NEIL: You don't know a damn thing about the relationship between me and my father.

T C: I know you haven't heard one word from him since he left.

NEIL: Which has just *got* to be why I've been searching for father figures ever since, right?

T C: You're the one on the rebound.

NEIL: Oh, is that what you think this is?

T C: No, I—

NEIL: 'Cause if it is, then fuck you very much.

(NEIL *and* T C *seethe at each other for a moment. Finally, T C gets up.*)

T C: I've gotta go.

NEIL: Yeah, you do that. 'Cause it's way past your Cinderella-assed curfew and Daddy's waiting up for you. Or maybe it's your homophobic stepmother. That witch who's young enough to be your baby sister.

T C: Yeah, that's right. She's just dying to convert me with her straight-assed magic wand. Meanwhile, you can jet on back to the club and hook up with some dark knight of your wet dreams who, unlike yours truly apparently, will be just oozing with fucking self-confidence and gay pride.

(T C exits, slamming the door behind him.)

NEIL: Shit, shit, shit!

(Lights fade to black.)

Scene Seven

(Lights come up on the Montgomery living room. T C is standing U S at the mantel talking on the telephone.)

(It's the same day, a little before 12 noon.)

T C: But we haven't checked out yet....

(EDDIE enters S R with his backpack, dressed the way he was in Scene Three. He goes to the entrance to the house.)

T C: How do you know he's not coming back? Some people leave their key at the desk because they don't want to... Oh.... Yes, just charge another day to my credit card. I have to keep the room, just in case he, that is, I—

(EDDIE rings the doorbell.)

T C: Wait a minute. *(He looks toward the front door hoping that it's NEIL. Into the phone)* What?... Yes, yes, I'm keeping the room.... Thanks. Goodbye.

(T C goes to the front door. He opens it to the double shock of seeing EDDIE there instead of NEIL.)

EDDIE: Man, oh, man. If it isn't Mister Tyrone Clarence Montgomery. T C from D C.

T C: Eddie?

EDDIE: Yeah.

T C: What the...Eddie?!

EDDIE: Yeah, yeah.

(EDDIE enters and the brothers hug each other tightly, almost for dear life.)

T C: This makes no— That is, how—? Where the hell have you been, man? All these years. I mean, the last I heard you were in Spain somewhere, but— Hell, some people just assumed you were dead or… I don't know. Dammit, Eddie, what the hell, man? Shit, I'd kick your butt if I thought I could.

EDDIE: You probably can now, little bro'. You probably can.

T C: Man, is it great to see you!

EDDIE: Same here, same here. Had no idea who'd be around. Just thought I'd tool on by to see the old neighborhood, maybe check in on the ole man.

T C: But how'd you hear about Dad? Hell, you didn't even bother coming home when Mom— *(With anticipation)* You… you do know about Mom, right?

EDDIE: Yeah…I know.

T C: I tried to find you, man, tried like hell. But nobody knew where you were. Not even Melinda when I tracked her down. I mean I thought you'd at least want to be in touch with your daughter, so your ex-wife must—

EDDIE: I know, T C. I've fucked up all around…. Look, none of it's on you, all right? It's all on me.

T C: How'd you find out about Mom?

EDDIE: Pure chance. A small item in the metro section of an old *Washington Post* I found stuffed under a seat on a train from Seville to Barcelona. Seven months after the fact. "First-term city councilman George Montgomery's wife of 39 years succumbs to cancer." Got off at the next little town. Spent that night in a sleepy ole bar near the train station, just drinking and smoking. Borrowed some money from a sympathetic ole codger and called home. I damn sure didn't wanna call collect. But when dad answered the phone I

couldn't bring myself to say anything. I just hung up.
Didn't know *he* was sick until I hit town a couple of
days ago.

T C: A couple of— So what the hell have you been
doing for two days?

EDDIE: Mostly sorta circling the airport waiting for
clearance to land.

T C: *(Nearly to himself)* I heard that.

EDDIE: How's the ole man doing anyway? I assume
he's at work. Never known anything to keep him
down.

T C: No, he's here. Upstairs sleeping. It didn't go so
well for him today with the radiation treatment. I told
Liz I'd look after him.

EDDIE: Liz. Yeah, I heard about her.

T C: From who?

EDDIE: Joanne Strickland. Well, she used to be
Strickland.

T C: From high school?

EDDIE: Yeah.

T C: Don't tell me you're staying with her.

EDDIE: Naw, naw, that'd be much too sweet to be true.
I'm...sorta hanging out in the park at the moment.

T C: You're joking, right?

EDDIE: Naw, the park's cool. Meaning it's not too cold
at night yet. And I'm an expert at bench-sleeping.
Know just how to place my head with my backpack
and my shoes under it for comfort and protection. And
don't worry about that hug we just had. Been washing
up in the men's room. Got my toothbrush and tiny
toiletries in this trusty little Ziploc plastic bag.

T C: Whole world in a backpack, huh?

EDDIE: The necessary stuff, anyway. Including my manuscript.

T C: Manuscript?

EDDIE: Yeah, all typed up, too. Courtesy of a brief friendship with a certain English-speaking Spanish lady.

(EDDIE *takes a manila envelope out of his backpack and gives it to* T C.)

T C: *(Reading the title page) Wayward Rocket* by Edward Montgomery.

EDDIE: Yeah. Wayward.

(T.C opens it up and flips through the pages.)

EDDIE: Shit, the manuscript itself almost went "wayward." In a not so surprising fit of jealous rage Mirabella tried to burn it one night. But I managed to rescue it just before I booked on outta there. Came back in search of a sympathetic publisher. It's set in D C so I figured…. Hell, what do I know? But then *you* do, right? Or you've gotta know somebody who does. Shit, I just knew coming home now was the right thing to do.

T C: *(Still looking through manuscript)* Damn, Eddie. I'm really impressed.

EDDIE: Shit, might not be much of anything really.

T C: Don't sell yourself too short yet. James Baldwin split for Europe with two Bessie Smith records and a typewriter and came back with *Go Tell It on the Mountain.*

EDDIE: I don't know about all that. Just trying to follow behind my little bro'. But then I've had lots of time on my hands. Both for writing and reading…. It was really hard at first. Bought this spiral notebook like I was in school again. When I filled it up, I bought another one. When I didn't have money, I used whatever I could "find". I'd gotten to thinking about things a few years ago when I came across this book in a used bookstore with a title that kinda grabbed me by the balls. *The Revolt of the Black Athlete.* Harry Edwards. Came out in 1970. But back then I was too busy being busy, too all up in it to be hip to it. Football, graduation, marriage. And me trying like hell to be one of those "terrific animals," which is what Edwards said one of his coaches called him almost to his face. *(A pronouncement)* Eddie Montgomery. The local boy with a rocket for an arm. N F L Draftee. George Montgomery's Legacy Son. *(Suddenly realizing)* That is—

T C: *(Giving manuscript back to* EDDIE) Hey, it's okay by me. Hell, I wish it was still true.

EDDIE: *(Putting manuscript in backpack)* I doubt that. I know you gotta be "in like flint". *(Going to the mantle)* Shit, I see Dad even took my football trophies off the mantel.

T C: He might want to be taking traces of me down off that mantel soon, too.

EDDIE: What do you mean? What's up?

T C: This friend of mine and I…. Well, we came to D C together and now I…

(T C just looks at EDDIE.)

EDDIE: What?

(Slight pause)

T C: I'm gay.

*(*EDDIE *just looks at* T C.)

EDDIE: I know.

T C: You know?!

EDDIE: Well, let's just say that I figured.

T C: But when? How?

EDDIE: I don't know, man. Mostly, I guess 'cause you've always only "sorta" dated girls, women.

T C: *(Laughing despite himself)* Hell, Eddie, I could almost say the same damn thing about a lotta guys. That doesn't make them gay, more like… inappropriately egocentric.

EDDIE: Yeah, well, I heard that. But then also I mean like you *were*, uh, *are*, my brother.

(Slight pause)

T C: Have you ever—

EDDIE: Nope.

T C: Nobody?

EDDIE: Not a soul. I figured it was your business, both to figure out and to put out.

T C: Yeah. *(Almost like a declension)* Put out, put out, and/or put out…. I want to come out to Dad.

EDDIE: Is he black? Your…

T C: Yes.

EDDIE: That'll help, I think.

T C: I don't.

EDDIE: Fuck it. Just do it.

T C: Just like that, huh?

EDDIE: Yeah.

T C: Just like you've been regularly faxing him your travel itinerary all these years.

EDDIE: Hey, let's not be getting into it over the courage factor unless you want me to be low-blowing you about Kathy.

(T C turns away.)

EDDIE: I'm sorry. That was already a low blow…. And now Mom's gone, too. *(Slight pause)* I paid a visit to her grave yesterday. Mom's. I just assumed she'd be buried next to Kathy. And there she was. And for a split second I stupidly wondered…wondered if there'd be any room for the three of *us*. You, me, and Dad. In whatever order…. Had to take the metro and then a bus and then walk to get there. But I'm used to that. Traveling without a car. Never thought that would ever happen after L A. But I've found out that it's the best way to sniff the air, suss out the lay of the land, see folks, get next to'em, finagle favors, odd jobs, warm beds, sometimes play the sexy, exotic, black American male card. It ain't all negativity and shit, you know…. Mom's got a nice headstone. "Alma Joyce Montgomery. Devoted wife, mother, and teacher. March 23, 1925–September 30, 1986. Now she sings with the angels."

(Slight pause)

(Finally, unable to restrain themselves any further, EDDIE and T C burst out laughing.)

T C: She wanted that last part. Her little "wink, wink," at those who knew that she couldn't…

EDDIE & T C: …sing to save her life.

(EDDIE and T C continue laughing for a moment, then turn reflective.)

T C: Seems like *September's* turned out to be the cruelest month of the year for our family.

EDDIE: *(Absently)* What?

T C: A variation on T S Eliot.

EDDIE: Who?

(T C lets it go.)

(Slight pause)

T C: She never really blamed you for what happened.

EDDIE: *(Unconvinced)* Yeah.

T C: She missed you so much.

*(*EDDIE *says nothing.)*

I didn't ask you to lie about it. I *never* asked you to lie about it.

EDDIE: It's all right, T C, okay? I did what I thought was right. Hell, you weren't even a double-digit dude yet.

T C: I just wanted to be the big brother for a moment. To stop feeling so mashed up in the middle for a moment.

EDDIE: I know, you knucklehead.

*(*EDDIE *playfully vice-grips* T C*'s head.)*

(Suddenly, the sound of a heavy object falling to the floor in the upstairs hallway is heard. EDDIE *and* T C *look toward the stairs. Then* T C *goes to the foot of the stairs.)*

T C: *(Calling)* Dad?

(There's only the sound of someone fumbling with an object.)

Daddy?

GEORGE: *(O S. Shouting)* It's all right, son. I'm all right.

T C: *(Calling)* Are you sure?

GEORGE: *(O S)* Yes!

*(*GEORGE *makes his way down the stairs. He's dressed in a suit and tie and carrying his briefcase, which, unnoticed by him, is open. At the landing he notices* EDDIE*, which stops him in his tracks.)*

EDDIE: Hi, Dad.

(Slight pause)

GEORGE: Who the hell brought you back from the dead?

EDDIE: It's great to see you, too.

T C: Eddie just got to town.

EDDIE: *(Setting the record straight)* Two days ago.

T C: He heard you were sick.

EDDIE: Two days ago.

GEORGE: Yeah, like he heard his mother was sick three years ago.

EDDIE: I'm…I'm really, really sorry, Dad. That was… that was unavoidable.

GEORGE: Her death was unavoidable?

T C: Daddy, don't.

EDDIE: You know what I mean.

GEORGE: Oh, like all the other things you've done over the past two decades of your life have been unavoidable.

T C: Do we have to get into this now? And are you going somewhere?

GEORGE: The Committee's voting on my housing bill this afternoon.

T C: I thought you were going to try to get it postponed.

GEORGE: That was Liz's suggestion.

T C: You agreed.

GEORGE: I changed my mind.

T C: But you've got to rest.

GEORGE: Look, I'm sixty-four, dammit, not a hundred and four.

EDDIE: T C's right. Don't those treatments sometimes—

GEORGE: You don't know a damn thing about cancer treatments, so you can just keep your mouth shut.

T C: Daddy, please.

GEORGE: All the ways it can catch you napping, all the different kinds of holes it can drill into you. You don't know about throwing up for the hundredth time and having to walk slow like you were some prematurely old woman. About your skin blotching up and your gums getting sore and your fingertips peeling off. About losing your hair and half losing your mind half the time. You don't know how all that sickness can twist a man all up inside, make him feel helpless and impotent and angry at the world to see his wife, the one person he loves more than anything in this world go *out* of this world just like that, almost as quick as his daughter did twenty-five years before. Like God was once again saying to the Montgomery family: "oh, well, y'all looking too good down there, too comfy, so—"

T C: Dad, stop! Please, just stop!

EDDIE: *(To* GEORGE*)* You think I didn't care about Mom? You think when I found out what happened I didn't wanna turn back the clock and leap clear across the Atlantic to see her alive again?

GEORGE: As far as I'm concerned you took that kind of leap in the opposite direction years ago.

EDDIE: Oh, like you haven't made a few leaps of your own from time to time. You did quite a bit of leaping yourself after I was born and pro ball kicked *you* in the ass 'cause, according to you, the league could only handle but so many Negroes at a time.

GEORGE: That was then.

EDDIE: And you were a quarterback with all that firepower and nowhere to aim it. *Then.*

GEORGE: I made it through law school.

EDDIE: While Mom worked her ass off to help keep food on the table.

GEORGE: Your mother was a saint.

EDDIE: Well, at least we see eye-to-eye about something.

GEORGE: And I didn't leave her and you by the side of the road like so much road kill like you did with your wife and child. I was working *my* ass off, too, and keeping my damn focus on the future. Not all the time being pissed off about the past.

EDDIE: Which means the reason you pushed <u>me</u> so hard just *couldn't* have been to try and make up for your own damn past, now could it?

(GEORGE *simply seethes.*)

EDDIE: And what do you care about my family anyway? You barely even know Melinda and Rachel.

GEORGE: Because you hardly brought them around.

EDDIE: We were clear across the country, and you didn't seem so eager to be making *that* kinda leap. It was almost like you were embarrassed to be seen with your white daughter-in-law and biracial—

GEORGE: Don't you lay that on me <u>or</u> your mother. That was and still is nothing but projection as far as I can see. *Projection!*

EDDIE: I *love* my daughter.

GEORGE: Then where is she now in your life? Where <u>is</u> she?

EDDIE: I'm in contact with her.

GEORGE: And when's the last time you *saw* her?

(EDDIE *has no ready answer.*)

GEORGE: 'Cause the last time *I* saw her was at your mother's funeral, when my "white" daughter-in-law at least had the decency to pay her respects. A beautiful young lady, that Rachel. With Alma's eyes, your mother's eyes. She was…almost what Kathy might have looked like at her age…. And then gone.

T C: Daddy, don't.

GEORGE: Gone!

T C: Please, don't.

GEORGE: Tore your mother to shreds. Shredded her. Kept her down and out for years.

EDDIE: Leave it alone, will you. For Christ's sake.

GEORGE: Gone! Just like you. No connections, no commitments, no respect for family or legacy.

EDDIE: Leave it alone!

GEORGE: But then hell, I should have known about you and responsibility the day Kathy was killed.

(For a split second no one moves. Then…)

EDDIE: *(Charging his father)* You son of a bitch!

(EDDIE grabs GEORGE around the neck, which causes him to drop his briefcase, some of its papers spilling out onto the floor.)

T C: Stop, Eddie, stop! You're gonna hurt him. You're hurting him.

(After a brief tussle, GEORGE manages to pull EDDIE's hands away from his throat. But now they're hand-to-hand, locked in what looks like some kind of end-game power struggle as they careen around the living room disturbing everything in their path. T C rushes around trying to wedge himself between them, but he's not as physically strong as either of them and keeps being forced back. Finally, as T C grabs at them yet again, GEORGE trips and falls and EDDIE

topples onto him hard, both actions propelling T C *away although he remains on his feet. As* GEORGE *and* EDDIE *wrestle to untangle…)*

T C: *(Yelling)* It wasn't Eddie, Dad! It was me! Kathy was holding *my* hand. Not Eddie's. *Mine.*

(Again, for a chilling moment none of the men moves. Then GEORGE *and* EDDIE *slowly get up,* GEORGE *rubbing his throat a bit. The silence is once again palpable.)*

*(*GEORGE *looks back and forth between* T C *and* EDDIE, *who are as much looking to each other as to their father. For his part,* GEORGE *seems rather disgusted with both of his sons now. He gathers his papers from the floor and puts them back in his briefcase. Then he quite deliberately straightens up even more, pulling himself up to his full height, and smooths out his suit. Finally, briefcase in hand, he gets his keys from a bowl on the mantel.)*

GEORGE: I've gotta go vote.

(Rubbing his throat and moving somewhat gingerly, GEORGE *leaves the house.* T C *and* EDDIE *remain speechless.)*

(Lights fade to black.)

END OF ACT ONE

ACT TWO

Scene One

(When the lights come up we see that the U R hotel room and the U L living room of JOANNE'*s house, along with the four-feet-high platforms, are gone and that the* MONTGOMERY *living room has shifted a couple of feet S R. Now visible in greater detail in the smaller space where the hotel room used to be is the front stoop of the* MONTGOMERY *home. In the larger space where* JOANNE'*s living room used to be is the enclosed back porch of the* MONTGOMERY *home. On the back porch are a chaise lounge and a couple of comfortable chairs.)*

(It is around six o'clock in the evening of the same day.)

(No one seems to be home. Then after a moment LIZ *enters S R carrying her purse and briefcase. She seems to have had a rough day. She comes up to the front porch and enters the house, closing the door behind her. She looks around, listens.)*

LIZ: *(Calling)* George? …T C?

(No answer. She sets her purse and briefcase on the table under the mantel and goes to the sofa and sits, taking off her shoes. Massaging her feet, she looks around again, this time as though re-assessing her place in the space. Then the telephone rings. She jumps up to answer it.)

LIZ: Hello…. Oh, hi, Joanne…. No, I still don't know how everything is 'cause nobody's here. I was sorta hoping you were George.... That meeting was over more than an hour ago.... No, you don't have to come over. I'll be okay.... Yes, I'm positive. Besides, like I said, Eddie's not here.... *(Laughing)* You can't fool me, girlfriend.... Yeah, I know that's right.... Yes, I will, I promise. Bye.

(LIZ hangs up and goes D L to the liquor cabinet. As she does, EDDIE comes quietly down the stairs U R, his manuscript in hand. He has just gotten up from an inadvertent nap. When he sees LIZ, he stops at the foot of the landing. He's taken aback by how striking she looks even from behind—perhaps especially from behind. He watches her with increasing interest as she bends down to open the cabinet, takes out a bottle of red wine, opens it, and pours herself a glass.)

(Still facing D S, LIZ takes a sip of wine and simply stands in deep thought. Finally, EDDIE clears his throat loudly. LIZ turns quickly, startled, nearly spilling her wine.)

EDDIE: *(Stepping toward her)* Hey, I'm sorry. Are you okay?

LIZ: *(Checking her clothes)* Yes.

EDDIE: Didn't mean to surprise you like that. *(Stepping toward her)* Are you sure you're—

LIZ: *(Begging him off)* Yes, it's all right, I'm all right.

(EDDIE stops, as LIZ, without realizing it, more diligently fusses with her appearance. Then she looks him up and down for a long, uncomfortable moment.)

EDDIE: I'd nodded off upstairs in my room. That is, what used to be my room.

LIZ: You look so much like your father.

EDDIE: So I've been told.

LIZ: I'm Liz.

EDDIE: So I've been told.

(Still clutching his manuscript, EDDIE goes to LIZ. They shake hands.)

EDDIE: Nice to meet you.

LIZ: Likewise. *(She takes a sip of wine.)* Would you like some wine or anything?

EDDIE: No, thanks.

LIZ: *(Putting the wine away)* I don't suppose that your father is also somehow magically upstairs resting.

EDDIE: Nope.

LIZ: Where's T C?

EDDIE: Probably out looking for his... *(Deciding to just say it)* ...for his boyfriend, I would guess. He apparently checked out of their hotel this morning. His boyfriend, I mean.

LIZ: Humph.

EDDIE: You don't like that word in that context, do you? "Boyfriend."

LIZ: No, what I don't like is the fact that T C seems to be neglecting his *father* for his "boyfriend." I would think that he— *(Eyeing EDDIE pointedly)* That *two* apparently grown sons could stop their father from seriously jeopardizing his health.

EDDIE: Yeah...apparently.

LIZ: At least one of you could have driven him to his meeting. And even waited to drive him back home if you had to.

EDDIE: If you think all that, then you don't know my father as well as you think you do.

LIZ: I know him well enough.

(Slight pause)

EDDIE: You still plan on getting married?

LIZ: I'm not going to dignify that question with any answer.

EDDIE: Meaning you're not so sure anymore.

(LIZ *hesitates, momentarily rattled.*)

EDDIE: I guess his prostate problems kinda threw you for a loop.

LIZ: Everyone's got problems.

EDDIE: Not in that area.

LIZ: I love your father.

EDDIE: *I'm* not looking to be convinced.

LIZ: And *I'm* not looking for advice from you.

(LIZ *simply stares at* EDDIE, *who smiles.*)

LIZ: *(Indicating manuscript)* What have you got there?

EDDIE: Chill, I ain't stealing nothing from the ole man. Although it's like a tornado or something struck all up in there. You been in there lately? Papers everywhere, file cabinets open, his old football memorabilia on daring display. He just up and took over my whole space like I was— *(He stops himself, somewhat embarrassed by his little rant. Then he simply shrugs and raises his manuscript.)* It's my life. I was fiddling with it upstairs.

LIZ: *(Eyeing it more closely)* Pretty thick. Must be pregnant with meaning.

EDDIE: *(Shrugging again)* It means whatever it says.

(EDDIE *sets his manuscript on the coffee table. Then he moves past* LIZ *and goes to the liquor cabinet, where he takes out a bottle of Scotch and proceeds to pour himself a drink, straight up. Meanwhile, she takes the opportunity to watch him from behind with interest.*)

EDDIE: T C tells me you're from Anacostia, too.

LIZ: Shipley Terrace.

EDDIE: Off Alabama?

LIZ: Yes.

EDDIE: We were on Shannon Place, between Nichols Avenue and the railroad tracks.

LIZ: Near that big ole Curtis Brothers chair.

EDDIE: Bingo. "The World's Largest Chair." When I was a kid, whenever I'd pass that chair I'd fantasize about sitting up there in it, looking out over all of Anacostia, D C, America, the whole damn—

LIZ: M L K Avenue.

EDDIE: What?

LIZ: Nicholas Avenue is called Martin Luther King, Jr. Avenue now.

EDDIE: Yeah, I know that. Since the revolts of '68. But when we lived in Anacostia it was called "Nichols," the name of the first head of Saint Elizabeths Hospital.

LIZ: Oh really?

EDDIE: Yep. I bet you don't know what it was originally called either.

LIZ: No, I don't.

EDDIE: Asylum Road. You see, the hospital was founded in 1855 as the Government Hospital for the Insane. They built it way on out of the city up on this hill across the Anacostia River. So far away, in fact, that when folks took the boat and then the carriage to visit their "unfortunates", they had to plan on spending the night. They say it was wounded Civil War soldiers who started calling it Saint Elizabeth's, after the colonial name of the ole hood, 'cause they didn't want to admit they were being care for in an insane asylum.

In 1916, Congress finally agreed and officially changed the name.

LIZ: I'm impressed.

EDDIE: *(Indicating manuscript)* Background for my life…. I suppose you went to Ballou.

LIZ: Class of '71.

EDDIE: Is that right? That's the same class my sister Kathy would have been in.

(LIZ says nothing.)

EDDIE: Except not at Ballou. Or Anacostia. We'd moved by then. I myself went to Coolidge.

LIZ: Just like Joanne.

EDDIE: Yeah, outta her zone. Lucky for me. But we all started out in Anacostia.

(Again, LIZ says nothing.)

(Raising his glass)

EDDIE: Here's to the Anacostian Diaspora.

(LIZ cautiously tips his glass.)

LIZ: She's been looking for you, you know.

EDDIE: *(Covering)* Who?

(LIZ simply purses her lips.)

EDDIE: Oh, you mean Joanne.

LIZ: Thought you were staying with this friend of yours. Warren, is it?

EDDIE: You seem to know a lot.

LIZ: I've been around.

EDDIE: Meaning here, of course. Not…the other thing.

(LIZ just looks at EDDIE for a moment.)

LIZ: Are you always this rude, or do you just flat-out have it in for me? What, you think I'm looking to cut you out of your father's will, or something?

(EDDIE laughs.)

EDDIE: I'm sure I've already managed to do that pretty much on my own.

(The telephone rings. LIZ sets down her glass and answers it.)

LIZ: Hello…. George! Thank God. Where *are* you? … Yes, I heard. Congratulations. So where are you? …You shouldn't be drinking. You know you've got another treatment tomorrow morning. When are you coming home? …You want me to come get you? …Okay, okay. It was just an offer…. All right, you be careful…. That's rhetorical, right? …Good. Bye.

(LIZ hangs up.)

EDDIE: Good ole Pops. Well, at least you know he's still on the planet.

(LIZ gives EDDIE a look.)

LIZ: I brought some work home with me, so if you don't mind… .

EDDIE: No problem.

(LIZ gathers up her shoes, purse, and briefcase.)

LIZ: If it's dinnertime for you, well, you know where the kitchen is. *(She goes upstairs.)*

EDDIE: *(To himself)* Yes, I do believe I do.

(EDDIE downs the rest of his Scotch. He picks up his manuscript, stares at it, and then lets it drop back to the coffee table in frustration. He takes a nearly empty pack of cigarettes from his shirt pocket, takes out a cigarette, and then takes a small lighter out of his pants pocket. He starts to light up and then remembers where he is. Lighter and

cigarette in hand he exits the house onto the front porch. He lights up, smoking as though he's been trying to quit and this is the first cigarette since the morning. After a few puffs, there is the sound of a car pulling up. He stares curiously S R, then half smiles, stubs out his cigarette, and waits.)

(After a moment, NEIL enters S R carrying a suitcase. He stops a "safe" distance from EDDIE.)

EDDIE: Can I help you?

NEIL: Uh…I'm looking for T.C…. Tyrone Montgomery. Does he live… is he here?

EDDIE: No.

NEIL: Oh, I'm sorry. *(Taking a piece of paper out of his pocket and referring to it)* I must have written down the wrong address.

EDDIE: No, you've got the right address, all right. He just ain't here at the moment.

NEIL: *(Confused at first)* But I— Oh, I see.

(Each of them waits for the other to say more.)

EDDIE: *(Referring to NEIL's suitcase)* You planning on moving in?

NEIL: *(Setting down the suitcase)* Oh, no. I… That is, I just took a cab from the airport.

EDDIE: Yeah, I couldn't helping noticing the cab.

NEIL: I didn't want to leave my suitcase there and I didn't think I could go back to the hotel because—

EDDIE: *(Mock surprise)* Oh, hey, wait a minute…. You're him.

NEIL: Yes…I mean, I think so…that is, who?

EDDIE: The guy who skipped out on T C.

NEIL: Well, um…he told you about me?

EDDIE: Yep.

NEIL: Oh.

(Slight pause)

EDDIE: Are you even twenty-one?

NEIL: *(Without thinking)* I'll be twenty-eight next month.

EDDIE: You one of T C's students or something?

NEIL: Oh, no, no, never. I've never been his student.
I'm a graphic artist.

EDDIE: Graphic...

NEIL: Artist.

EDDIE: Uh-huh.

(Slight pause)

NEIL: We met at a taste of Chicago concession stand in
Grant Park a couple of summers ago. He'd come down
from Evanston. He teaches at Northwestern. Oh, but
then you know that. Anyway, I lived, *live*, near the
park. It was such a beautiful day. Great breeze coming
off the lake. He was ordering a polish sausage, which
was just what I'd gotten and he made this comment
about good ole ethnic Chicago. At first I didn't even
know he was talking to me. And when I did I got sorta
embarrassed. But then he laughed and I laughed and
we decided to...

*(Realizing that he's been going on and on and that this
man he assumes is T C's father has simply been staring and
listening, NEIL suddenly trails off.)*

NEIL: ...sit down and eat lunch together. Anyway
that's how we met.

EDDIE: Uh-huh.... And you do *graphic* art.

NEIL: *(Sensing EDDIE's meaning)* Well, not "graphic"
in that way necessarily. Hardly. Ever. *(Impulsively
defensive)* I make a decent living at it. *(With a laugh,
stupidly trying to recover)* Okay, I know the cliché about

gay men in artistic fields, but I was also on the high school wrestling team for a year.

EDDIE: Oh, the crotch-attack sport.

NEIL: *(Embarrassed)* I ran track, too. All through high school. Sprints.

EDDIE: That must have come in handy.

(Further unnerved, NEIL is speechless. EDDIE laughs.)

EDDIE: Hey, I'm just messing with you. I've played all kinds of sports, so I've probably seen more male crotches up close than you by a long shot.

(NEIL isn't sure how to take that comment. EDDIE grows more serious.)

EDDIE: Are you...are you "in love" with T C? Or are you just hanging out?

NEIL: No, no, sir, I...I love him.

EDDIE: Then why'd you book on him?

NEIL: Book?

EDDIE: Split, leave.

NEIL: Because he wouldn't— *(He is at a loss for how to proceed.)* That is, I'm just not...just not sure how much he loves me.

EDDIE: A whole lot, it seems to me. He's just sorta scared right now. But it's not like he's got some fatal disease. It's not even chronic, I don't think. Know what I'm sayin'?

NEIL: Yes, sir. That is, I think so.

EDDIE: Speaking of which, are you being safe? You know, because... well, you know.

NEIL: Oh, yes, sir. All the time, sir.

EDDIE: That is, are you...I mean, you're not...you know, that positive thing. That negative positive thing.

NEIL: No, sir. Neither one of us, sir.

EDDIE: Well, all right then.

(Slight pause)

(EDDIE steps up close to NEIL, which causes NEIL to take a tiny step back.)

EDDIE: Okay, so listen up. I've got just one more thing to say…. Don't you hurt him, okay?

NEIL: No, sir. I mean, no. I'd never do that.

(EDDIE gives NEIL a look that's crystal clear about his already having hurt T C.)

NEIL: That is—

EDDIE: Because I will always be T C's big brother. Know what I'm sayin'?

NEIL: *(Surprised)* You mean you're not his—

EDDIE: Naw.

NEIL: I'm really sorry, sir. I thought you were Mister Montgomery.

EDDIE: *(Mock indignation)* I *am* Mister Montgomery, boy.

NEIL: No, sir, I know, sir. I meant—

EDDIE: Hey, hey, it's okay, it's cool. Just relax…. For now. And you can stop with the "sir" stuff. *(He stretches out his right hand.)* I'm Eddie.

(NEIL takes EDDIE's hand somewhat warily. Then EDDIE smiles, which gives NEIL license to smile. Now they shake hands firmly.)

NEIL: Nice to meet you. I'm Neil.

EDDIE: Well, you've come this far. Might as well come on in.

(NEIL takes up his suitcase, but just then yet another sound of a car pulling up is heard. EDDIE and NEIL turn D R as a

car door closes. Then T C *enters from* D R, *clearly surprised to see* NEIL. NEIL *puts down his suitcase.)*

EDDIE: *(To* T C*)* Look who I found.

T C: Yeah, I see.

NEIL: Hi.

T C: Hi.

EDDIE: Where the hell have you been all afternoon?

T C: Downtown, checking out the sights, mostly on the Mall.

EDDIE: What for?

NEIL: Must have been looking for that white guy.

*(*T C *smiles.)*

EDDIE: What white guy?

(Neither NEIL *nor* T C *answers.)*

EDDIE: Okay. Something tells me I wouldn't wanna know anyway. *(Picking up* NEIL's *luggage)* I'm taking this inside.

*(*EDDIE *goes into the house.* T C *and* NEIL *continue to stare at each other.* LIZ *comes down the stairs with anticipation.)*

LIZ: Is that George?

EDDIE: Nope. T C and Neil. *(Putting down* NEIL's *luggage)* They're staying the night.

*(*LIZ *says nothing.)*

EDDIE: In the meantime, I've got *me* some serious work to do now.

*(*EDDIE *gets his manuscript from the coffee table and heads* U L *to the kitchen.)*

EDDIE: Oh, and if it's dinnertime for you, don't worry. I'm gonna be out on the back porch, not in the kitchen.

(EDDIE *exits into the kitchen.* LIZ *looks toward the front
door, sighs, and then goes to the bar. She will pour herself
another glass of red wine and pace some in the living room,
still worried about* GEORGE, *during the following scene
between* T C *and* NEIL. *At the same time,* EDDIE *will come
out onto the screened back porch with his manuscript, take
out a pen, and sit down to do some work.*)

NEIL: This feels kinda stupid.

T C: What does?

NEIL: Me standing here like I'm barring the door to
your own house.

T C: Well, since you're so buddy-buddy with my
brother now—

NEIL: I thought he was your Dad.

(T C *bursts out laughing.*)

NEIL: Oh, you think that's funny?

T C: No, no, it's not you.

NEIL: He had me almost peeing in my pants.

T C: That would have been some sight.

NEIL: Now you *are* laughing at me.

T C: I'm sorry.

NEIL: Leave it to you to leave it to me to have to—

T C: Hey, I didn't plan this, all right? Besides, look at
it this way: you got a chance to rehearse, perfect your
game.

NEIL: Is that all this is to you?

T C: Will you stop. (*Slight pause*) Thought you were
going home.

NEIL: Then why were you on the Mall?

T C: Wishful thinking. Would have been like winning
the lottery, I guess.

(NEIL *and T C just stare at each other for a moment. Then* NEIL *goes to* T C *and they hug and kiss. Then* T C *pulls away, suddenly mindful of where they are.)*

T C: I'm really sorry.

NEIL: For what? Kissing me out in the open like this?

(T C *purses his lips.)*

NEIL: *(Tenderly)* Me, too.

T C: Come on in.

(T C *and* NEIL *enter the house.* LIZ *turns to them.)*

(Pause)

LIZ: *(To* T C*)* So you're really going to do it.

T C: Yes. No choice.

(Slight pause)

LIZ: *(To* NEIL*)* I'm Elizabeth Hall. Liz.

NEIL: Neil Russell.

(LIZ *goes to* NEIL *and they shake hands.)*

LIZ: Would either of you like a drink?

T C & NEIL: No thanks.

(Slight pause)

LIZ: Well, looks like we'll be ordering in again.

T C: We could all go out. My treat.

LIZ: No, your dad's been out enough all day.

(There's yet another sound of a car pulling up. They turn with anticipation toward the front door. Even EDDIE *looks up from his manuscript, then and gets up and enters the house with it. During the next short beat* GEORGE *enters D R and heads for the front porch, briefcase in hand, weaving a little from too much drink, looking somewhat disheveled.)*

LIZ: He doesn't need any more stress than he's already put *himself* through.

T C: Look, I don't—

LIZ: Plus, he's got his treatment in the morning.

T C: We don't intend to be keeping him up.

(EDDIE enters from the kitchen with his manuscript.)

NEIL: *(To T C)* I'm sorry.

T C: Don't be.

NEIL: Maybe I should just go.

T C: No.

NEIL: But if—

T C: No.

EDDIE: 'Sides, it's too late for that now. Way too late.

(At the front door GEORGE sets his briefcase down and fumbles noisily with his keys. Everyone looks toward the front door. LIZ goes to the door and opens it just as GEORGE tries to put his keys in the lock, causing him to stumble a bit. Meanwhile, EDDIE has placed his manuscript on the rectangular table under the mantel.)

GEORGE: *(Immediately straightening up)* Hey, sweetheart.

LIZ: George. Look at you. Are you all right?

GEORGE: *(Picking up his briefcase)* Of course, I'm all right. *(Entering)* Hell, I'm more than all right now.

(T C and EDDIE step toward GEORGE, but NEIL moves further away, almost as though he'd suddenly like to disappear.)

LIZ: *(Looking out the door)* Where's your car?

GEORGE: *(Mumbling)* I left it.

LIZ: *(Closing the door)* What do you mean you lost it?

GEORGE: *(Emphatically)* I said I left it.

T C: Then how did you get home?

GEORGE: *(Laughing)* I beamed myself up.

T C: Seriously, Dad.

GEORGE: I got a ride from a friend. Somebody I met. *(To* LIZ*)* A *guy. (Back to everyone except for* NEIL, *whom he's yet to notice)* Working class dude. Native son like me. Post Office. Mail carrier. Carried him right on into the middle class. Just like it's done a lotta black folks in this town. We got to talking about all kinds of stuff, the Masons, which he'd just joined, the crack epidemic. Got a cousin hooked on that mess. And football, y'all, when he found out I'd been a Q B back in the day. Blasts from the past. He'd heard of'em all. Fritz Pollard, Willie Thrower, Warren Moon. And my man Doug Williams airing it out for the Skins last year in the Super Bowl. Also told him about the housing thing, of course. Had to collect me another loyal constituent. Always on the campaign trail. So time just flew right on by…. I'll get my car in the morning.

EDDIE: Hope you can remember where you left it?

GEORGE: *(Angrily)* Didn't I just say that I didn't lose it? You never listen. Never have listened to me really. Even when I tried to school you about reading defenses. Always too impulsive, too prone to go with the first option. Two and three, I'd tell you. Keep an eye out for two and three, too. That's probably one reason you washed outta pro ball so damn fast. All that opportunity down the drain with the Drano.

(While EDDIE *seethes,* GEORGE *turns to* LIZ.*)*

GEORGE: I did it, baby. *Me.* My damn bill is finally out of committee, which makes it close to a sure thing now. And Congress better not be layin' a hand on this one. I'm gettin' tired of them crackers treatin' us like we were some third world protectorate.

LIZ: Honey, listen—

GEORGE: Yes, indeed, Marion's got nothing on me today. *I'm* the man today.

LIZ: That's great, honey. Why don't you—

(LIZ *tries to get him to sit down but George resists, pulls away, refuses to be corralled. Dropping his briefcase on the coffee table, he's now riffing on his own logic and memories.*)

GEORGE: I told him not to worry. Told him I'd handle it. Our constituents. Gonna transform ole Barry Farms again, give it some proper play again…. Shoot, Barry Farms, all right. It *was* the Barry family farm, you know. This white couple, that is. That's who the Freedmen's Bureau bought it from after the Civil War. Buy some land across the river. Sell plots on time to up and coming black folks. Raise a bit of money for the newly chartered Howard University. Win, win, win situation…. The Barry's farm. Then we moved the "s", some damn body moved the "s". Hell, you know how we black folks love to be choppin' off the "s's" in our possessives. "Barry farm." Then Barry Farms. And now it's almost like Marion Barry's farm. Barry's farm team morphing into Ward Eight. *(Excited)* Wait, wait, listen to this: "Marion Barry's Ward Eight David and Julia Barry's Farm." Get it? "Barry's Ward *Ate* Barry Farms." *(He laughs.)* How's that for Anacostia history in a nutshell?

(*Although others may get the pun, no one else laughs.*)

LIZ: Listen, honey, why don't you sit down at least.

GEORGE: I've been sitting down in that bar all evening, Liz…. Anacostia. Shoot, I came up there. Lotta folks did. Had me a rocket for an arm, too. Do you know what it's like to have a rocket for an arm and then all of a sudden not be allowed to use it? All that firepower and nowhere to aim it. Can you imagine how much it hurts? Your arm getting hot and heavy like it was some kind of sealed up cannon just aching

to explode. You know, when I was younger—not that
much younger, mind you 'cause I ain't that old. But
when I was younger I'd sometimes dream my right
arm was so humongous I couldn't even lift it. It'd get
bigger and bigger and bigger until it'd sorta push the
rest of me right on outta the bed. Plop. It's a wonder it
didn't just role on off the bed and crush me to death.
A man's gotta be able to use what he has, boys. Use
whatever firepower he has. Your mother knew that,
rest her sweet soul. Alma understood where I was
coming from. Always understood. But it seems like
y'all don't seem to know it all of a sudden. If you ever
did. *(Specifically to* T C *and* EDDIE*)* Just look at you. The
two of you. But where's my daughter, my little girl?
Where's Kathy? How come she ain't here? Bet you
understand that. Know about that. *(Another memory)*
Armstrong High School. Yeah, baby, I was the "Strong
Arm of Armstrong." *(He laughs.)* I was *it* at Armstrong,
just like my brother had it going on in his head at
Dunbar. As for *Anacostia* High right nearby? Well, you
see, white folks claimed it was much to "high" for us
coloreds back in the day. *(Drifting more)* Private homes,
though. We had us some private homes. Middle class.
Ole Frederick Douglass looking over us up on Cedar
Hill. And when integration came along we showed'em,
didn't we, Alma? Showed'em how we could spread
out, make it out. And now they wanna be squeezing
the rest of us outta that good ole housing stock close in
town. Capitol Hill striving like hell to be a mountain.
(A pronouncement) "Chocolate City melting in the
noonday sun of gentrification." *(More focused again,*
building) And that damn Councilman Pierce having the
nerve to condemn me for compromising, for so-called
"trading gay rights for housing rights." Hell, I've got
a right to trade on it. We been traded on and traded
on and traded on for far too long. So he better not be
gettin' all up in my face like that. I do what's right

for black folks. To hell with his queer ass. He and all
his AIDS-spreadin' constituents. Talkin' about how I
promised to stand with him. Well, I stand with black
folks first! Black folks and morality! Always have,
always will.

(No one says anything as GEORGE *looks toward* LIZ. *Then
he goes to her.)*

GEORGE: I'm sorry, Liz.

LIZ: It's okay, honey.

GEORGE: I didn't mean to go off like that.

LIZ: It's okay. You just need to get some sleep.

GEORGE: Yeah, it's been quite a day. But tomorrow I'm
gonna take you out, I promise. A celebration dinner.
Just the two of us.

LIZ: Good. But let's see how your treatment in the
morning goes first.

GEORGE: *(Wheeling away from her)* No! I don't need
another damn treatment. Don't you understand?
Haven't you been listenin'? How come nobody around
here's listenin' to me? I'm a man, I tell you. A black
man. I am goddam George Alvis Montgomery. Got
me a rocket for an arm. All that firepower and finally
somewhere to aim it. And that's what they don't like.
A black man with firepower and the balls to use it. The
guts, the will. 'Cause firepower plus willpower equals
one dangerous-assed B M I C. Black Man in Charge.

(As GEORGE *laughs and swirls around again, he notices*
NEIL *for the first time.* NEIL *smiles faintly.)*

GEORGE: Hey, wait a minute. Wait one a minute.

*(*GEORGE *focuses closely on* NEIL. *The tension in the room
rises.)*

NEIL: *(With a tentative wave)* Hi, sir.

GEORGE: Don't tell me I've got a grandson I don't know about. Now I know I've got me a granddaughter, but— *(Pointedly to* EDDIE*)* Damn, boy, you been holding out on me?

(Before EDDIE *can say anything,* GEORGE *staggers severely.)*

LIZ: Oh, my God.

*(*EDDIE *and* T C *rush to him and grab him to keep him from falling.)*

EDDIE: You've gotta go upstairs to bed, Pop.

GEORGE: Naw, first I wanna be introduced to my grandson.

EDDIE: Later.

GEORGE: Don't be so rude now. Hell, I won't bite. *(Stepping toward* NEIL*)* Hey, grandson. *(To* EDDIE*)* Maybe he'll be taking up that mantle you threw down. *(Back to* NEIL*)* Although he's kinda on the scrawny side.

T C: He's not Eddie's son, Dad.

*(*GEORGE *now focuses on* T C.*)*

GEORGE: Don't tell me he's *yours*. Well, hell's bells. You secretly married? Or did you just—

T C: No.

GEORGE: "No" to which of the above?

T C: He's…

GEORGE: Come on, come on, spit it out. *(Spinning around to everyone)* He's always had trouble spitting things out. So quiet, so shy. But an ace student. Brains for days. Alma's doing, I think. Her genes flowing. Although I'm no slouch it that depart—

T C: *(Blurting it out)* He's my boyfriend.

GEORGE: *(Stopping in his tracks)* Say what.

T C: This is Neil, Dad. Neil Russell. And he's my boyfriend.

(GEORGE *eyes* NEIL *up and down.*)

GEORGE: Your boy...

NEIL: (*Anticipating*) I'll be twenty-eight next month.

GEORGE: ...friend. Boyfriend. As in...

(*Slight pause*)

T C: I'm gay, Dad.

(*Slight pause*)

GEORGE: You're gay.

T C: Yes.

GEORGE: *You're* gay.

T C: Yes.

GEORGE: You're a...a homosexual.

T C: Yes.

GEORGE: Since when?

T C: Sorta since birth, I guess.

(*Suddenly,* GEORGE *isn't sure who to focus on.*)

GEORGE: What, is this some kind of a joke? You got Councilman Pierce hiding out in a closet here or something?

T C: No.

GEORGE: (*Ranging around the room*) What the hell is this then? What in God's name have I stepped into, come home to? I go out in the world to do my thing, make important decisions, be who I am to all kinds of folks, secure myself, and then come home to all this? I mean this morning wasn't bad enough? ...*Two* sons all up in my face, in my way, with their, their...*crap.* Laying all kinda crap on me when all your behinds

had to be doing was listening to me from time to time,
to me and your mother from time to time, follow
some examples, hold up, hold on to some traditions,
to what family is. What the black family is, or should
be, what a black *man* should be. Responsibility, ethics,
morality. And then bring it on home, bring *that* on
home. Hold on to *that*. Not none of this who-struck-
John crap…. Two sons. Two lost sons. Lost *boys*. Some
damn Peter Pan shit. Tinkerbelle and fairy dust and
fantasies about "finding yourself." And so who am
I, huh? Captain Hook? You spittin' at me like I'm
some kinda lame-assed crippled old man you plan
on throwing overboard to the goddam alligators?…
Shit, both of you. Round and round and round in the
damn wilderness when all you had to do was get your
act together and bring it on home. *(Pointedly to* EDDIE*)*
Come straight home! *(Pointedly to* T C*)* Or at least come
home straight!

T C: No! Stop it! Don't say that. Don't you be sayin'
that to me.

EDDIE: T C, don't—

T C: Because I tried. I *tried*.

EDDIE: You don't have to explain nothing to—

T C: *(Pressing on)* I…I tried shrugging it off, throwing
it all off. All that "girl's room" stuff. Shit, no, I mean
…. A regular boy. Just a regular boy. But I felt, I was
beginning to feel …. But no, uh-uh. No… Besides,
I was busy. Especially after Kathy…after she died.
I was busy. Busy being good and polite and smart
and studious…. Wild Eddie. Always out there. Like
a god. Some damn god. My big teenage brother with
all those trophies and all those girls, clinging to him,
calling him up. Eddie. It's for you, Eddie. Pick up the
phone, Eddie. Eddie, can you …. Was okay. I didn't
understand but it was okay. Mom's baby now. She had

me still. Cause you had Eddie. Mirror image. George
the second. And I'd look in the mirror and see, see…
just me. A me I didn't always wanna see because ….
But then who could I ask? Who would understand, or
even care? Shit… Study, read, do my work, be good.
Boy Scout motto to the max. Keep me on the straight
and narrow. But what did that mean? What the hell
did that all mean to me? …So don't you dare…say that
to me. Come home straight? Don't you… I can't…

(T C has exhausted himself. NEIL *goes to him.* EDDIE,
*furious, grabs up his manuscript from the table under the
mantel and throws it down in front of* GEORGE, *possibly on
the coffee table next to* GEORGE's *briefcase.)*

EDDIE: *(To* GEORGE*)* There! It's all I've got…. You
wanna know why? You wanna know who, what,
when, where, and how? …There! *(Speaking with sober
intent)* It was in my head for so long. Stuffed all up in
there. Pounding, taking up space, sucking up oxygen,
keeping me awake all night and then sending me
crashing down. Like some sorta…hallucinogen. Like
when I'd do mescaline back in the day. Tripping for
hours that seemed like seconds and then sleeping for
more hours that stretched on like days. The glaring
sun, then the stars and the moon. Over and over and
over again like a cycle that never seemed to wanna
take me along with it. And I'd pace up and down and
up and down whatever confine, whatever little room,
whatever space I'd secured, commandeered, carved
out of someone else's place—some woman's, or even
some admiring guy's. Me. The expatriate, the black
power figure manqué. Shit, the powerless figure just
black and lost in a string of cities, towns, villages, a
badgering bunch of foreign languages taunting me,
teasing me. Languages which I never studied, didn't
have to study, 'cause in school I was so cool, a star
athlete just like you, Dad. Until suddenly, one night in

some dim light in, in, shit, I don't know. Switzerland,
I think, the pressure had built up so much I was either
gonna die right there or let it out, open up some
hidden door and just let it all pour. And I took up this
pen and grabbed this pad I'd been using to calculate
my expenses, my allotment for the day, my figuring
out how much I was gonna have to beg, borrow, or
steal to get through to the next night, and I wrote... I
fuckin' wrote in big bold capital letters: "I SEE D C."
(Pause. Indicating his manuscript) I was gonna try to do
something with that. Something. Letter to the world
or some such shit.... But now.... Shit, I don't fuckin'
know.

*(EDDIE gets his backpack from behind the sofa and heads for
the front door. T C goes after him.)*

T C: Eddie, wait. Don't go. *(Moving back and forth
between EDDIE and GEORGE)* Dad? ...Where're you
going? ...Dad, don't let him— ...Eddie, stop. Don't go.
You don't have to—

*(EDDIE exits onto the front porch and keeps walking until
he disappears S R. No one seems to know what to do now,
what to say. GEORGE stares somewhat bewilderingly at T C.
Then he looks at NEIL, and lastly at LIZ. Finally, weaving a
bit, he picks up his briefcase, deliberately ignoring EDDIE's
manuscript, and begins heading for the stairs. LIZ follows
behind.)*

LIZ: *(Touching him)* Here, I'll help you.

GEORGE: *(Jerking away)* No!... I don't need your help.
Don't need you to be puttin' me to bed. I know where
it is. I know what to do when I get in it, too. *(With a
curious look)* Why you wanna be bothered with me
anyway? Bothered with any of this? Besides, I don't
need me no more kids, least of all sons. Not if they're
gonna turn out like the ones I already got.

(GEORGE *goes shakily up the stairs. As he exits, all* LIZ, T C, *and* NEIL *can do is stare after him.*)

(*Lights fade to black.*)

Scene Two

(*Dim lights up on the living room. It's three o'clock in the morning of the next day, and* GEORGE *is sitting D R in the easy chair and staring into space. He's dressed in his pajamas, robe, and slippers. He looks drained. Beside the easy chair on the floor, half hidden from view, is* EDDIE's *manuscript.*)

(*After a long moment,* LIZ *comes down the stairs. She wears a nightgown, robe, and slippers.* GEORGE *senses not only that someone is there but that it is, in fact,* LIZ, *but he doesn't turn to her.*)

LIZ: I knew by about the third time you inadvertently kicked me that you couldn't sleep. Least I think those kicks were inadvertent. How long have you been down here?

(GEORGE *says nothing.*)

LIZ: Eddie come back?

(*Again,* GEORGE *says nothing.*)

LIZ: T C and Neil are—

GEORGE: I know where they are.

(*Pause*)

LIZ: You know, I really used to believe in the lyrics of that old Marvelettes song. (*As she speaks, she continues down the stairs and fully into the living room.*) Especially when I was just this ten year-old dancing around to it in the living room, pushing my two little brothers aside 'cause they always seemed to be in my way, all up in my business. This time they were taunting: "Lizzie's

shakin' her bootie, Lizzie's shakin' her bootie." "Don't
call me that. My name's Elizabeth. I am Elizabeth."
That's what my father insisted on calling me, anyway.
Elizabeth. His princess on the way to being a queen.
And then Mama, his West Virginia gal, would grunt
and bop him over the head. "Hold your horses," she'd
say, "I ain't gone nowhere yet." *(Singing)* "There's too
many fish in the sea." *(Back to speaking)* Daddy *loved*
to fish. Ate it up. He'd go with his buddies whenever
he could. Fish off of Hains Point or in the Chesapeake
Bay, sometimes in the Atlantic. Wear his pea-green
lucky hat and Baltimore Bullets jacket. Mama hated
fishing, almost never went. Boats made her seasick real
easy. She also hated the mess he made in the kitchen
whenever he came back with a big catch. Scales all over
the place, guts in the sink, fish eyes staring up at you
every which way. But boy, did she love to eat them
after he'd fried them up. We all did…. I went fishing
with him some. He liked taking me along, even just
the two of us a couple of times before my brothers
were old enough. He'd made each of us our own little
fishing poles out of finely smoothed down wood and
eye hooks and empty spools from Mama's sewing
basket. He could make anything. Think it, see it, make
it…. When he passed, just keeled over with a massive
heart attack when I was in college, he almost took my
heart with him. *(Singing)* "There's short ones, tall ones,
fine ones, kind ones. Too many fish in the sea." *(Back
to speaking)* One time me and my brothers came home
with something like three dozen fish between us. We
were so happy. And Mama was so… "let me get out
y'all's way while you get to cleanin'." But then other
times there'd be only two or three. Or none. "'Sokay,"
Daddy would say, "'cause didn't we have a good time
anyway?" *(Singing)* "Too many fish…" *(She just looks
at* GEORGE *for a long moment.)* You think I only wanna
marry you so I can have kids? 'Cause I damn sure

don't need you for that…. Too many fish in the sea, my foot…. There's only you. Straight up. No rhetoric. *(She goes behind the easy chair and hugs* GEORGE *from behind.)*

GEORGE: I read it. *(Indicating the manuscript)* Eddie's "manuscript." His book.

*(*LIZ *notices the manuscript on the floor for the first time. She picks it up.)*

GEORGE: *Wayward Rocket*… Funny. I half expected it to be about me…. But no, it's Eddie, all right. His life. Wandering, searching, questioning, trying to find a home. Like this here suddenly somehow wasn't one for him. Still and all… Hell, I don't know. I think it's halfway good. Or at least honest…. At one point he says…says he thought he was the only dumb person in the family. That if he didn't make it as a professional ballplayer he'd be sunk. "What if I hit a brick wall like my Dad did? What if I get hurt?" He wasn't me, he wasn't his mother, he wasn't his brother. So who the hell, what the hell was he gonna be? *(Slight pause)* Huh…. "A brick wall."

*(*GEORGE *looks out as* LIZ *continues holding the manuscript.)*

(Lights fade to black.)

Scene Three

(Lights come up. It's mid-morning of the same day. T C *and* NEIL *sitting on the back porch. In the living room* EDDIE's *manuscript is back on the rectangular table under the mantel.)*

T C: Me and Eddie used to have a great ole time on this porch. Getting into all kinds of things. Good and bad. That is, when he wasn't out with his "boys". *(Slight pause)* I called Joanne, his old girlfriend, but he's not there.

(EDDIE *enters S R carrying his backpack. During the following beat between* T C *and* NEIL, EDDIE *will come to the porch, start to ring the doorbell, but then decide not to. He'll turn back as though to go and then take out a cigarette and light up, smoking. Meanwhile* GEORGE *will come down slowly from upstairs, dressed casually. He'll look around, go to the table and pick up* EDDIE's *manuscript, then put it down, restless, almost uncertain what to do next.)*

T C: Eddie and Joanne. They were so tight, so in love. Hell, I was sometimes more jealous of that than all the big-time athlete stuff. *(He gently touches* NEIL.) One time when he was in high school he told me how Joanne was even gonna help him study at the last minute for this big history test. He said that this time he was actually going to at least "C" a test. And he didn't mean see one for the first time. He meant get at least a "C" grade. My big, bad brother. *(Slight pause)* I miss him already…. Hell, I've missed him most of my life, it seems. What if he's gone for good this time?

(This time NEIL *gently touches* T C.)

(There is a moment of silence as EDDIE *smokes,* GEORGE *looks out, and* T C's *question lingers in the evening air, unanswered.)*

NEIL: What'd he get on that test?

T C: A "C plus."

(Suddenly resolved, EDDIE *stubs out his cigarette and rings the doorbell. Both* GEORGE *and* T C *get up to answer it,* GEORGE *going to the door and* T C *exiting into the kitchen,* NEIL *following him.* GEORGE *opens the door to* EDDIE. *They stare at each other for a moment as* T C *and* NEIL *enter the living room from the kitchen.)*

EDDIE: I came back for my manuscript. It was sorta stupid of me to just leave it here.

(GEORGE *steps aside, lets* EDDIE *enter, leaving the door open.* EDDIE *goes to the table and gets his manuscript, putting it in his backpack. There is an awkward silence.)*

EDDIE: I'd swear this neighborhood has gotten a tad more "chocolaty" since I was last here.

T C: Where'd you stay last night?

EDDIE: Doesn't matter…. Take good care, baby brother. You, too, Neil. I like you.

(EDDIE *and* GEORGE *look at each other for a moment. Then* EDDIE *heads for the door.)*

GEORGE: You captured your mother pretty well.

(GEORGE'*s comment stops* EDDIE, *although he doesn't turn back.)*

GEORGE: Some of her quirks and habits. The way she liked to dance around a room, liked to socialize, organize events, parties, get-togethers. The way she had a taste for living out life through all her senses, her need to give, her constant "aim to please". *(He looks around the room.)* She's the one who picked this house. We'd had a couple of other options but she just came down those stairs and spun around this room like she was seeing all the possibilities and said: "Yes!"… And so I said: "Okay." *(Pause)* Stay… Please.

(EDDIE *turns back into the room and looks at* GEORGE. *Then he makes a decision to stay, closing the door.* GEORGE *turns to* T C *and* NEIL, *focusing specifically on* NEIL, *who suddenly becomes immensely self-conscious and embarrassed.)*

NEIL: Uh…well, you know, I can—

T C: It's all right.

NEIL: Yeah, I know. But…I can…upstairs. My sketch pad's upstairs so I can…. *(He exits up the stairs.)*

(GEORGE looks back and forth between EDDIE and T C for a moment.)

GEORGE: Do you know why neither one of you is a junior? 'Cause truth be told your mother wanted a junior. She had this weird thing about legacy. There're a fair number of juniors on her side of the family, you know. Uncle Charles, your great Uncle William, cousin Aloysius. Huh, poor kid. But I put my foot down. Both times. Because I had my own weird wish. I wanted to be sure that you'd go beyond me, above me. I don't know. Call it ego if you want. Not wanting you to be "burdened" by the possible weight of my name. Huh, ego. Wherever I go…ego…. And now I see that there was this other kind, too. The kind that just assumed that enough of the best parts of me, whatever they were, would always be in you without me having to name them, announce them, put a label on them…. My sons. *(He stares D S away from his sons.)* My children. *(After a long moment…)* Tell me what happened that day. The truth of it all.

(Both T C and EDDIE know that "that day" refers to the day Kathy was killed. T C also knows that it's he who must answer.)

T C: It was like a thousand nails scraping across a blackboard. And then suddenly she wasn't there. Kathy wasn't there. And everybody was screaming and I smelled gasoline and saw smoke. I turned to get away and got knocked down and somebody fell on top of me and my book bag slid away and I was thinking, "my lunch, they're gonna crush my lunch and Mom's gonna be mad." And now people were *crying* and screaming. And when I sat up I saw her further into the crosswalk. He legs were twisted funny and her favorite

blue skirt, the one she wished she could wear to school
every single day forever, was now blue and red and
was up over her waist, which made me embarrassed
for her. But I couldn't see her face. It was turned away
from me. And I wanted her to get up. I kept telling her
to get up. Just get up. But she wouldn't get up. And
I screamed for Eddie. And he seemed to come out of
nowhere. He held me and said don't look, T C, don't
look. And then he let me go and ran over to Kathy,
and the crowd just seemed to swallow them up…. And
later when the ambulances came, before you and Mom
came, I just kept crying and telling Eddie that I didn't
mean to let her go, I didn't mean to. But then he said,
"No, T C. It was *me*. Don't you remember? It was me
who let her go." And I didn't understand. What was
he talking about? He hadn't even been around. But still
I nodded. I just kept nodding and nodding. 'Cause he
was my big brother and knew a lot more than me. I
kept nodding and nodding and nodding until…until it
became true. I just let it be him, let it be Eddie.

(EDDIE *knows that that's not the whole of it, that he must
try to complete it for both* GEORGE *and T C. He puts down
his backpack.*)

EDDIE: I saw the terror in his eyes, Daddy. The terror
in T C's eyes. It was screaming at me louder than
anything I was actually hearing. (*Slight pause*) You and
Mom always told me to walk Kathy and T C to their
school before heading out to mine. But that day Bubby
and Dennis and Weegie were hanging around, sorta
tailing me, joking around with me. They wanted to go
to the yard to sneak in some basketball before school
chewed us up and spit us out one more day. And
then T C said he could do it, that he was big enough. I
wasn't sure but he kept on begging me and my friends
kept on pulling at me. Ball, ball, let's play us some
ball. So finally I said okay. Told him to be careful and

to keep hold of Kathy's hand. And he said that he would, promised that he could. And they went on.... He was so proud of himself. Walking his little sister to school. My big little brother. *(He takes a moment.)* One. Two. Three. I've been counting those steps for almost thirty years. Sorta like a quarterback's drop-back and quick release. One, two, three, release. One, two, three, release. You always said I had one of the quickest releases you'd ever seen. Only I wasn't quarterbacking yet, so I wasn't looking. Just turned to go, so happy to be going. One, two, three, and then the sound of a car skidding, like it was coming at me.

(Pause)

GEORGE: *(Almost to himself)* Life.

(There is a sense that, although the three men are in same space, each is grappling alone with the last thing that GEORGE has said. Finally, for the first time, GEORGE seems to truly lay himself out nakedly before EDDIE and T C.)

GEORGE: I'm scared, boys.... Your ole man is really scared.

(GEORGE slowly goes to the sofa and sits down in its center. At first T C and EDDIE don't seem to know what to do. They're hesitant about approaching their father, as though each were waiting for the other to take the lead. Then finally, simultaneously, as they now seem to be on the same page looking at the same cue, they awkwardly head for the sofa. They sit on opposite ends of their father, EDDIE on his right and T C on his left. Then EDDIE takes GEORGE's right hand in his left and T C. GEORGE's left hand in his right. They sit like this for a moment, without inhibition. Then GEORGE lets go of their hands and wraps his arms around EDDIE's and T C's shoulders, holding them tightly.)

(Lights slowly fade to black.)

END OF PLAY